FATHER

ST. AUGUSTINE ACADEMY PRESS
HOMER GLEN, ILLINOIS

KINO / Priest to the Pimas

by ANN NOLAN CLARK
illustrated by H. LAWRENCE HOFFMAN

NIHIL OBSTAT:
Rev. William F. Hogan, S.T.D.
Censor Librorum

IMPRIMATUR:
✠ Most Reverend Thomas A. Boland, S.T.D.
Archbishop of Newark

The nihil obstat and imprimatur are official declarations that a book or pamphlet is free of doctrinal or moral error. No implication is contained therein that those who have granted the nihil obstat and imprimatur agree with the contents, opinions or statements expressed.

This book was originally published in 1963 by Vision Books, a division of Farrar, Straus & Company, Inc.

This facsimile edition reprinted in 2019 by St. Augustine Academy Press.

ISBN: 978-1-64051-085-2

Author's Note

THE FACTUAL ACCOUNT of Eusebio Francisco Kino is accurate and follows the events of his adult life as written by him in *Favores Celestials*.

Little is known of his boyhood other than the place of his birth and data obtained from church records and memories from those members of his family who still reside in the original Kino home. These memories have been written by Bolton who is considered an authority on Kino.

Description of lifeways and folkways of the villages and the people of the Tyrol at the time of Kino's boyhood I have obtained from many sources. It is impossible to furnish a complete bibliography because I did most of my research reading during a four-month stay in the hospital and many people brought me everything they could find concerning Jesuit history, Kino history and articles and descriptions about that part of Europe where the young Kino lived and received his religious training. I read also early accounts of Mexico, California and Arizona and checked maps of the period, many of them copies of the ones Kino had made. At a later date I traveled over the territory of Mexico and California where Kino had lived and worked and visited many of the early mission sites.

Besides the many people of Santa Fe who gathered source material for me, I wish to thank my brother, Carl Nolan, who interested me in writing about Father Kino, Dr. Bergere Kenney, who fostered the idea; Mabel Parsons, Phoebe Nolan, the Morrows, and my hospital nurses, who made "bed-reading" possible for me, and the Santa Fe librarians who sent for all the books. I also wish to thank Sister Jean Catherine of Loretto Academy, Santa Fe, for bringing me magazine articles about Tyrol traditions; Father Joseph Clark, S.J., Brigham City, Utah, who suggested books about the Jesuit Order; and Father McDermott of Brophy College, Phoenix, Arizona, who checked the final manuscript.

An incomplete bibliography follows: *The Spanish Borderlands, Rim of Christendom, Kino's Historical Memories of Pimería Alta, The Padre on Horseback, Jesuits on the Pacific Slope, Rivers in the Sun, Spanish Explorations in the Southwest,* and *Outposts of Empire,* all by Bolton; *Educational Foundation of the Jesuits in Sixteenth-Century New Spain* by Jacobson; *Jesuits in Mexico* by Dunne; *The Jesuits* by Campbell, and *The Origin of the Jesuits* and *St. Francis Xavier,* both by Brodrick.

Father Kino, Priest to the Pimas

Chapter 1

THE BOY LOOKED UP the stony slope that bordered the side of the road away from the river. This was the place he had planned to reach. This was the time he had planned to reach it. A glow of thankfulness lighted his heart. It was always to be this way, all through his life. He would dream and plan, and if his plan succeeded he would allow his heart its beat of thankfulness.

Earlier this morning, in the cold gray of

before-the-dawn, he had left the loved, warm hearth-fire of home. For a long time he had been dreaming of this day, of this spot, of the hour when he would reach it. He had estimated the time it would take.

He had begun his journey slowly, steadily, in the Tyrol way of walking. Slowly, steadily he had walked across the empty square of the village, by the village church of Santa Maria, by the house of his godparents and the houses of his neighbors. Quickly he had left the village behind him and walked along the river road to the narrow opening in the valley, his valley, the Vol di Non. Slowly, steadily, as always with people of the Tyrol, his feet had talked with the ground. The ground had answered them. Now he was here.

Leaving the road, the boy climbed up the stony slope to a wayside shrine only partly hidden by the trees around it. The mountain slopes and canyons were dotted with shrines, toy-sized chapels, and high carved crosses where the lonely Christ hung crucified. This wayside shrine, although little different from others around it, was a special one to the boy. Always at sunrise he could see it distinctly from the dooryard of his home in the valley below. For this reason he had planned to get here at sunrise time. If he could see the shrine from his home, he reasoned, he could see his home from the shrine. Reaching the shrine, he knelt, bowing his head. The wooden Mary above him smiled down her blessing.

At the moment of his kneeling, the great bell in the village below rang out the sunrise Angelus.

For as long as the boy could remember, his village church bell had directed his days. At sunrise it rang for morning prayer, for breakfast and for work beginning. At noon it rang for mid-day prayer, for food and rest. The herdsman, the shepherd, the laborer in field and orchard and vineyard, knelt at its clanging and prayed together. Then the wives and mothers and sisters came walking together, bringing deep bowls of hot, thick soup to their workers. The sweetest Angelus was at evening time. It was then, after prayer, that all the villagers walked contentedly along the narrow trails to home, to supper and to sleep.

The boy was used to Angelus—it marked his day into its parts—but this morning's bell seemed different. It seemed a calling forth of promise, a heralding of a beginning. He listened joyfully to its majestic clang. Its sound was clear and strong. No other bell in all the world could sound so powerful and so beautiful. Its splendor filled the valleys and the canyons. It swelled in majesty, then stopped. The clanging stopped. It did not die away in echo, nor melt into the mountain walls. All sound was cut off clear and sharp. The world was stilled with listening.

The boy's voice broke the silence around him. He said his prayer aloud, as he had been taught to say it.

"The Angel of the Lord declared unto Mary. . . ." The Ave Maria which followed was but a whisper trailing the memory of the great bell's clang.

Again the bell rang out. Again it stilled.

"Behold the handmaid of the Lord," the boy prayed. "Hail Mary, full of grace. . . ."

The air was cold, as sparkling pure as the Alpine snow on the mountain peaks that pierced the sky. For the third time the bell rang its Angelus. For the third time it became silent, giving man his turn.

". . . and dwelt among us," prayed the boy. ". . . now and at the hour of our death."

The glory of the rising sun descended until at last it touched the hands of the wooden Mary of the wayside shrine. It touched the boy's jaunty hat, and his cheek. Creeping downward, it lay across the stone-filled road.

Many sunrises had touched this old road that had been old before the birth of Christ. Even in that ancient time the Vol di Non had been clustered, much as it was this day, with tiny hamlets in each mountain fold. The boy was not thinking of the sunrise, nor of this age-old road which Roman merchants had traveled on their way to Brenner Pass, gateway to the Tyrol. He was not thinking of the people who had lived in this valley before Christ was born. He was thinking of tomorrow, his tomorrow and the new life it would bring him. Because his thoughts were of tomorrow, he remembered yesterday, his yesterday.

This had been his plan. Here, where he could see his home, he would say good-by to it, greet tomorrow, and bid farewell to yesterday.

The boy finished his prayer. Slowly, deliberately he walked to the edge of the slope and he looked down on the road that crossed the length of the Vol di Non. A thin flow of people traveled its rocky way. Some rode horseback. A few were in horse-drawn pony carts and wagons. Most were walking. Tyrol folks were born to walk. They never hurried and seldom rested. They walked to their fields and their pastures, their vineyards and orchards. They walked to their village church. They walked through the days and the years and the centuries. There was nothing to break the timelessness of their walking except church and chores, worship and work.

No one noticed the boy this morning as he stood on the edge of the slope looking down into the deep distances. He looked much like the other travelers—slight, sturdy, strong. He was dressed as many of them were dressed: jaunty hat with a feather, black shorts, wide embroidered belt, short jacket, heavy, homespun stockings, heavy mountain walking boots. Only the colors of the embroidery on his belt and stockings gave hint to the identity of his village. Only the size and shape of the bundle he carried gave hint as to why he was here.

If a stranger had noticed him, he would have said, "The boy is Italian from the village of Segno." This was true. He would have said, "The boy must be a traveler. See the bundle he carries." This also was true. But no one could have guessed from the smallness of the bundle that the boy's journey was to be a lifetime long and his destination a world away.

No one looked at the boy, nor did he look at anyone.

Below him lay the Vol di Non cupped in the folds of majestic, towering mountains, heartland of the Alpine world, his home. The Vol di Non was a rich basin. It had no plains, no low curving hills, no softening outlines. It was mountainous, rough, torn, canyon-filled. But every canyon had its valley, and every valley had its Tyrol village. The floor of the basin was dotted with them. Past every village, curving and twisting in its rocky bed, the River Noce flowed to join the mighty Adige. Along its banks ran the river road from Brenner Pass to Trent.

The boy gazed down on the villages. Never before had he seen them like this, laid out in pattern. Soon he was able to pick out Torra. Torra was part of home, for there he had been baptized in the Sant' Eusebio Church. Segno, his own village, had its own church, Santa Maria, but it was not as large as Sant' Eusebio nor did it have a baptismal font nor a resident priest. So the boy, the only boy in a houseful of girls, had been baptized at Torra. The father, Don Francisco, and the mother, Donna Margherita, had seen to this. On the day of his birth he had been taken to Torra for his baptismal ceremony, a journey on his first day of life. It may have marked him with the traveler's urge.

The boy's aunt, Donna Rosa, and his uncle, Don Eusebio Kino, were his godparents. They gave him the name Eusebio, the same as the church and his godfather. Eusebio Kino. Thus he was to be known in the Tyrol of northern Italy, in the great colleges of Upper Germany, in many medieval cities of Europe. Thus he was to be known in a far-distant land.

For as long as he could remember, Eusebio Kino had loved Saint Francis Xavier. Early in life he had given this saint his complete devotion. No matter where Eusebio was or what his work, Francis Xavier guided him, directed him, comforted him. Today, looking down at Torra, his thoughts turned inward. He examined his heart and it seemed as if Saint Francis spoke to him.

What about the Company of Jesus, the Jesuits? Did he want to be one of them? He thought he did. He knew that he wanted to travel. The world beyond the brooding Alps called him, pulled him, urged him to come. Did he want to go as a Jesuit? Did he want to go as Francis had gone, among the poor of the world, giving comfort to their bodies and hope to their hearts? He thought he did.

His relative, Father Martin Martini, had been a Jesuit. Traveling through China, converting its people, he had grown to know the Chinese people and be loved by them. His books on China had earned him the reputation of a scholar, while his work had earned him the respect due a beloved missionary. Father Martini was remembered with pride in Segno. What he had been and what he had done was told and retold to the Kino children. He was their good example, their model—much more so than another relative who was of noble blood, who had left his title of nobility, his lands and houses to the ancestors of Eusebio's father.

The Kino parents were well-bred and well-to-do. Because they were leading citizens of their village, they felt great responsibility to it. Because they owned land, they felt it their duty to make it yield richly. To be known as a family who worked hard and worshipped with devotion was more important to them than holding a noble title. To have happy hearts and souls at peace was more important than to have noble blood. They were sturdy folks, thrifty and God-fearing. Italians of the northern Tyrol are not as fun-loving nor as carefree as those of the southland, for life in the Tyrol is hard. It takes fortitude to live in a land where seven months of the year are snow-filled and every night is cold with frost.

Eusebio's father had pastures and fields, orchards and vineyards. He labored in them for fruitful harvest, his family at his side. Eusebio, young as he was, knew about growing grains and raising cattle. He knew how to prune the fruit trees and pick the grapes.

Tyrol life, rustic and work-worn though it was, had a splendid freedom and a splendid faith. There was only one master, the God who held in His hands their days and their destinies. So Don Francisco taught his son. So taught Father Arnoldus, resident priest of Torra, visiting priest of Segno.

Father Arnoldus had been old when he had baptized Eusebio, and now he was very old. His hair was white, his step slow. But his words were as forceful as ever and his insight as keen. It was Father Arnoldus, teaching Eusebio his catechism and his books, who had discovered the boy's remarkable mind and his ambition. He knew of Eusebio's wish to go beyond the mountains, his uncertain thoughts about becoming a Jesuit priest.

Father Arnoldus was certain that the boy had a vocation to the priesthood. The first preparation for this must be education. The boy must have learning strong and undiluted. He must be sent to the well-springs of wisdom, the colleges. As the father toiled for the yield of his land, so must the son be taught to toil for the yield of his mind.

The old priest talked to Eusebio's parents. He told them these things which he had been thinking. The parents were not against an education for their son. They were eager for it and eager that he should become a priest, if God called him. For this end they made their sacrifice. They would send him away to school. They loved him, their only son, and they needed him, but they bade him go. They blessed him and sent him on his way.

Deliberately, slowly Eusebio's gaze found Segno. He found Santa Maria Church, his house, his home. The pain of saying good-by to it was a knife in his heart. Family and village life were all that he knew, for in the Tyrol a man's village *is* his life. Since the time of Christ, Tyrol people have fought and died to keep their land their own. Family ties are close and strong.

Eusebio thought of the long winter months

when his family gathered into itself in safety and happiness. He thought of his family's house that for hundreds of years had kept storms outside and family love within. He thought of the great beehive stove where the family gathered when winter storms were raging. Here he had learned his prayers and the rules for a good life. Here he had learned to honor God and to keep His laws.

The Kino mother had told her children of the lives of the saints. There were many saints to tell about, as many as there were days in the year. Eusebio had come to know them as well as if they walked beside him on the mountain trails. He had learned to love them for their gentleness and their goodness. He wished he could be like them, bringing bread to those who hungered, offering the cup to all who were thirsty.

The Kino father had told his children of the fighting men of the Tyrol. Eusebio had come to know them as well as if he had fought beside them in battle. He knew their strongholds, the castles that crowned the rocky pinnacles that guarded every glen. He had learned to respect these fighting men for their love of freedom and of home. He wished he could be like them in their courage and their daring.

From the Kino grandparents the children had learned the songs of the Tyrol. They had learned the dances, the festivals and folkways of their village. Eusebio had learned to yodel and to dance the ceremonies of harvest and of planting time.

Around the beehive stove in the long Tyrolean winters a bond was woven and strengthened and tightened, binding the boy to his family and to his village. Now he was breaking this bond.

But he need not hasten the breaking. He need not tear the home-ties thoughtlessly. He would do it slowly, with gentleness and with love. He would remember for a moment each thing that was dear to his heart. He would remember each thing by itself and completely. Then, having given it the moment of remembrance, he would lay it aside—perhaps forever, he did not know.

Tonight, when his family was eating the evening meal, he would not be there. As clearly as if it lay before him, Eusebio pictured the family room. He saw the heavy-beamed, low ceiling. He saw the great stove and the benches around it. He saw the bare, heavy plank table and the crucifix on the wall above it.

Tonight his family would sit at this table. As clearly as if he were there, he saw them. At one end was his mother's chair. At the head of the table, opposite her, his father sat. To his left sat his daughters and the women who worked for him. To his right sat the men who worked for him. Only one seat would be empty, the one at his right hand, nearest to him. This was the son's seat. It would be empty. Eusebio would not be there.

Hanging on the wall by the stove was a leather strap with thongs threaded through it. To the thongs were tied the wooden spoons, one for each family member. In his mind Eusebio could see the spoon strap plainly. One spoon, only one spoon, would be left hanging there: his spoon, for he would not be there to use it.

He saw his mother bring to the table the large wooden bowl filled to the brim with thick hot soup and fat hot dumplings. The family would serve themselves. One portion would be left: Eusebio's portion, for he would not be there to eat it.

In his remembering Eusebio heard his father say the blessing for the evening meal. It was a short grace, said distinctly and with dignity.

God and family must hear the food being blessed.

The boy remembered last night. There had been family prayers and family tears. At dawn this morning there had been family tears and family blessing. Eusebio had not cried. He was too old, too manly to cry. He had stood gravely and silently while his mother and his sisters wept. He and his father had touched hands briefly, but without words. They had not said Good-by.

This remembering was the boy's farewell. It was his good-by to home. Slowly, deliberately, completely he remembered all the small things he held most dear. Slowly, deliberately he remembered them and put them aside. From this hour on, he promised himself, thoughts of home must be a luxury to be afforded briefly.

In the time to come, thoughts of home must have whispered to his heart as he walked the silent corridors of colleges and the silent trails of strange and dangerous lands. But if they did, they were only whispers, never in words that were spoken aloud.

For a heart-heavy moment, the boy stood looking down into the valley. Then quickly he turned away. Quickly he climbed down the rocky slope where the wayside shrine of the

Virgin stood partly hidden by the trees around it. Quickly he reached the road and mingled with the other travelers. No one noticed him. He was but one of the travelers among the many who walked the road.

Eusebio Kino followed the noisy River Noce as it wound its way through the Vol di Non to join the flooded deep Adige. Slowly, deliberately he walked along the road. If his feet talked to the land as he hoped they would, he would arrive at the gate in the city wall of Trent. He would get there by evening Angelus.

The year was 1661.

Chapter 2

THE GATES IN THE WALL of the city of Trent were still open when Eusebio reached them. At his back lay the Vol di Non misted in the evening shadows.

The boy did not look back. His gaze was on the open gates in front of him and on what lay ahead, inside the city wall. Around him the steady stream of travelers flowed under the age-old arch. Eusebio went with the crowd.

Before his wondering gaze lay a medieval city rich in history, in learning, in ancient castles, in majestic churches, in splendid sculpture and in works of art. Before him lay a city proud, old, cultured—a different world from simple, rural Segno.

All kinds of people milled around him. He could pick out the soldiers and the pilgrims. Who the others were, he did not know. Each man wore the traditional costume of his calling, his village, his country. Each man spoke his mother tongue.

Trent belonged to Germany, but its laws and customs were Italian. The languages spoken on its streets were as many as the people who spoke them. Eusebio spoke Italian and German and a dialect which was a mixture of the two. He had also a smattering of Latin which he later perfected. Learning languages was never a problem to Eusebio Kino, as he was to find out in the years to come.

Now, as he walked along in the twilight of evening, he was not listening to the conversations of his fellow travelers. His ears were closed to the sounds around him. Only his eyes were aware of the sights of the city. The monuments in the squares, the towers, the many buildings delighted the boy from the village of Segno. Everything he saw was bigger, grander than his dreams had been. For this he had been praying for as long as he could remember. He had been waiting to become a part of this. To live here in this great city, to learn all that it had to teach him had been his heart's deep wish.

He was not too excited, too interested, too busy to say a prayer of thanks to St. Francis Xavier. Then he stopped to ask the way to the Jesuit college. There he would spend this night and many nights. There he would stay, he thought, until his hunger for learning was satisfied. Beyond this he did not know.

The streets he walked along were narrow, crooked, paved with cobblestone. He thought them wonderful. Around the city loomed towering mountains, encircling and protecting it, but Eusebio gave neither glance nor thought to them. He was used to mountains. It was the streets and the buildings that excited and delighted him.

At last he reached the Jesuit Residence. He was received at the outer gates. No bells rang to welcome him; he was one of many asking for entrance, begging for learning. They came every day and the gates were opened for them.

The boy, at this time, was in his early teens. He was sensitive and shy, but he had the courage to combat his shyness. He had the will to hide his sensitivity. But his life-way was not formed at this age. He had neither years nor experience to help him. He had only dreams and promise, only faith and strength. These were what he brought with him to Trent.

The college at Trent was as different a world from the home at Segno as the streets of Trent were different from the mountain trails of the Vol di Non. It was different in every way.

The college world was a world of strangers. Students from all over Europe attended classes and lived there. To the boy of the Tyrol any person not of his parish was a stranger. He was not to be accepted quickly nor lightly. Every little village in the Tyrol was complete in itself, isolated and content with its own isolation.

The college world was a world of strangers and a world of men. The home at Segno had overflowed with women: the mother, the sisters, the women who worked in the house and vineyard. Eusebio was used to the ways of women and to the things that they did for him. It was a simple home where the father was head of the house. But all the men of the house were respected because they were men. The women took care of them and did things for them. They looked up to them. In a way, they served them.

As the only boy in a family of girls, the son, the heir, Eusebio was used to being served. It was customary and right. He accepted it without thought. When he did not have it, he missed it, without knowing what it was that he missed.

The college corridors were long and shadowed and silent places. The college cells were bare of all small comforts. There were no down-filled pillows or feathered ticks on the beds at the college. The beds were pallets. Though the house at Segno was a rural house, simple and plain, it was bright and warm and comfortable and filled with the joyful noises of family living. There were no shadowed, silent places.

Food on the college table was scanty and poor, prepared and eaten with indifference. It was not made up of mellow cheeses, ripened fruits, purple grapes nor the rich thick stews of home.

It must have been very hard for the Tyrol

boy to accept the ways of the Jesuit college. Eusebio Kino was to lead a dedicated life, but such dedication must have been learned slowly and painfully. Every step which he took into the new life opening before him must have been slow, deliberate and difficult.

It did not take Eusebio long to make the pattern of Jesuit life his way. In the Tyrol village of the Vol di Non there had been Mass and Vespers, song and prayer to honor God. But here God was not only the Father, He was Life. In Segno, Eusebio had walked with God and obeyed His laws, but here at the college this was not enough. Now he tried to lead the life that Christ would have led had He walked the streets of Trent in the year 1661. Once prayer had been a part of his day; now his day became a prayer.

Eusebio had loved Francis Xavier with a boy's devotion. Now he loved him as one who was determined to follow his footsteps across the world. Young though he was, Eusebio turned his thoughts to this end. His ambition extended beyond the Alps and the life of a scholar. It reached into the heart of the world.

Comfort and food became important only because the doing without them could be offered to God as a small bouquet. This doing without became habit, a part of Eusebio Kino. His later life became noted for his indifference to hardships, to hunger and to thirst.

Strangers became no longer strange. They became brothers. The instructors at the college came to share the place in the boy's heart with his Kino family. They did not take the family's place but enlarged the family to take in their world.

The love the Jesuits had for each other and for the boys in their care was for Eusebio as sunshine is to a plant. There grew within him a strength, a peacefulness, a sweetness and an understanding that was to last him throughout his life. Not only were the Jesuits gentle men, they were powerful and forceful teachers. Not only did they touch the soul and the heart of Eusebio Kino, they explored and developed his mind. Under their teaching, Eusebio's eager curiosity, his hunger for knowledge, his promise of brilliant scholarship outgrew the college of Trent and what it had to offer.

At the end of the second year, he was sent to Innsbruck and Hall for further training. Innsbruck was the capital of the Tyrol. It lay to the north of Trent on a wide green plain on the banks of the River Inn. Surrounding the city were the jagged peaks of the Dolomites which, although a part of the Alps, were unlike other Alpine mountains. They rose from the vivid greens of the plain's grasslands, the light greens of the larch forests, the somber greens of the pines, to the ash-gray bare rock peaks that tore the sky. No one could live in nearness to the powerful Dolomites and not be influenced by their awful majesty. So must the young Eusebio have been influenced, perhaps without being aware of it or especially noticing the grandeur of his surroundings.

The city of Innsbruck was old. It had been a market place on an ancient crossroad when the Romans conquered it before the time of Christ. Since its beginning it had grown rich from men who traveled the Brenner Pass with their marketable goods.

Hall, across the river, had also a history ancient and proud. Its wealth had come from its salt mines and it was known as Envy of Princes. Its castles were elaborate, much more so than the ones on the mountain pinnacles of the Vol di Non. The most important one was almost a village in itself. Wherever Eusebio looked, he must have seen its many-sized buildings, dormer windows, overhanging balconies and belfry towers which brooded over the city. It must have given him a sense of belonging, of being a part of an old, old pattern which had outlasted the centuries.

Hall had many magnificent churches and a famous convent. For hundreds of years this convent had been loved by the ladies of royalty. To its quiet halls they had come for prayer and peace, leaving it lavish gifts in thanksgiving for their hours of solitude. The convent had become famous for its rich possessions, its jewels and laces. Its vestments were stiff with gold embroidery. Its altar of solid ebony inlaid with silver was a delight to see. Eusebio must have seen this convent chapel many times. He must have seen its possessions of uncounted richness. Yet, young as he was, he must have had the ability to value things used for God's glory for the love they held rather than for their pricelessness. If this were not true, how could he have offered, in later years, with such love and pride, simple crosses made of palm fronds?

The university, renowned for its brilliant teaching staff, was both at Innsbruck and Hall. It was not long before these men recognized the outstanding promise of the new student from Trent and Segno. Eusebio in turn admired them, especially one Father whom he loved and trusted. He it was in whom Eusebio confided that at last he was certain beyond doubt that he wanted to be a Jesuit—a missionary, he hoped, to China.

Later in the year, Eusebio became ill. Some of the best physicians of Upper Germany were called to treat him, but he grew worse. As his Jesuit friend knelt at his bedside, looking down at the dying boy, he suddenly asked Eusebio why he did not beg his patron saint to pray God that his life be spared. For a long moment the priest was not certain that the boy had heard the gently-spoken question. He was so very ill, so very weak. At last Eusebio looked up. His lips moved in prayer, promising Saint Francis Xavier that if his life were saved he would ask admission into the Company of Jesus, to be sent as a missionary to work in foreign lands.

Eusebio regained his health and requested admission into the Jesuit order. After two years of interviews, questionings and examinations, he was admitted as a novice. He started on the long, long road of discipline and training.

The year was 1665, and Eusebio Kino began his novitiate at Freiburg.

For the next two years he was trained in the spirit and discipline of the Order which was to be the pattern of his life. He learned to master his will power, to temper his judgment, to perfect his patience, to love with wisdom and aid with compassion. He learned to walk the way of poverty, he whose early life had been as the son of the village land-holder. First, last, and always he learned that he must obey. To obey in all things was one of the vows Jesuits took to last until death released them.

The life of the novice was detailed and exacting and unending. Day by day, by month, by year the pattern did not change. Eusebio, with the other novices, rose before dawn and went to the chapel for prayer and meditation on a subject which had been determined the night before. The mind was not to be allowed to wander; it was being disciplined as well as the body. Mass, more prayer, and breakfast followed.

Breakfast over, the routine work of the day began. Eusebio worked in the fields and in the kitchen. He did heavy manual labor on the farm as well as the simplest of household chores. No task was thought too lowly because all labor was done for the glory of God. He was sent to the hospital to tend the sick and scrub floors. He went into the schools to teach the children. He went into the streets to preach to the people and into the prisons and among the poor to give help where help was needed. He was sent on a short mission without money or provisions of any kind, that he might learn firsthand how to walk with poverty. He must learn what it was to ask for a bed to lie upon and to beg for bread to eat.

Before Eusebio could rest, there were other things he must accomplish: scholarly and spiritual readings, conferences with the Master of Novices, lectures to hear, notes to take, and questions to ask and to answer. And there was the daily examination.

These things accomplished, there were Vespers, prayer and meditation and, if time permitted, sleep. Perhaps it was during these years in the novitiate that Eusebio Kino learned that sleep was a luxury, not a necessity. Sleep was something else that he learned to do without.

Eusebio made the thirty-day Spiritual Exercises which are the foundation of the Jesuit order. When he had completed this retreat, he took the three vows of the Company of Jesus and added Francisco to his name in honor of his patron saint. Now he would be known as Eusebio Francisco Kino.

About this time, his parents having died, he

willed to the Jesuit order the lands and properties they had left him, for "poor persons dedicated to God." He was now, truly, a man of poverty.

Eusebio was ready for additional training. As a Jesuit, he would have to be able to take his place in the world of letters. At the university in Ingolstadt, on the banks of the Danube, he spent the next three years, studying the classics, mathematics and philosophy. At this time Ingolstadt was considered the leading Jesuit college of Upper Germany. On its teaching staff were some of the most learned men of the century, including a mathematician and a cartographer. Under the brilliant instruction of these two men, Eusebio Francisco Kino developed amazing ability.

Because of his achievements in mathematics, the young man's boyhood dream of going to China was rekindled and renewed, for Jesuit mathematicians and cartographers had for many years been highly favored at the Chinese court. Early missionary Jesuits who had been sent to China had mapped the country, revised the Chinese calendar and translated scientific books for the use of Chinese scholars. Another gifted Jesuit would be welcomed by them. So the young man dreamed and studied and prayed for a mission to China.

He did other things, too. He begged other young missionaries who were being sent to the Orient to ask the Father General for Kino to help them in their labors. He himself wrote to the Father General in Rome for permission to go as missionary or in any other work that might be pleasing to God. He left no stone unturned. Everyone who had ever heard of him knew that he wanted to go to China.

After Ingolstadt, Eusebio was sent back to Hall for three years to teach at the university. His fame as a teacher must have been as widespread as his reputation as a scholar, for the Duke of Bavaria came to Hall to offer him a Doctorate in Mathematics at the court in Munich. He would have special court favors. This was a great honor to be offered to any young man, and a very great honor for the village boy from Segno. Eusebio Kino refused. He had set the goal for his life's work. It was not to be a favorite at the court of Munich; it was to be a missionary to a foreign land.

The year was 1677, sixteen years since the young Eusebio had walked the road from Segno to Trent. Sixteen years had passed, years of discipline, study, prayer and longing for permission to take the Word of God to those who had never heard it. The time had come to look back upon those years, and look forward into the future. Eusebio Kino was given a year to look backward, to look forward, to be sure of God's will before he made his final vows. For this important year he was sent to Ottingen. Ottingen was a new place for him, so there would be no memories to help him make his decision. There would be no friends, no loved instructors to distract or guide his thinking. He would be alone with God.

At year's end his decision was the same as it had been at the year's beginning. He would be a missionary. He would work in a foreign land. He hoped, he prayed, he thought it would be in China.

At Ottingen Eusebio Kino was ordained, made his final vows, and said his first Mass. Then came news, the news he had been praying for, asking for, waiting for during the past ten years. Permission had been granted. He was to do foreign mission work. But there was a problem. Two missionary fields were open— Asia and Mexico—and two young priests had been selected to go: Father Eusebio Kino and Father Antonio Kerschpamer. No one could decide which priest was to go to which place.

At last the young priests themselves decided how to solve their problem. On two slips of paper they would write "Asia" and "Mexico." Then they would draw. The slip they drew would decide for them.

Young Father Kino was not too excited. He had the ability, the knowledge and the training that was thought highly of in China. He had the desire and the courage needed for such a dangerous journey. He had the stomach and the strength for such a rough sea voyage. China would be his destination; he was sure of it.

One of the Fathers prepared the slips of paper and held them in his hand. The young priests drew. On Father Kino's slip the word "Mexico" was written. He would go to Mexico. God's will be done.

The year was 1677.

Chapter 3

GOD'S WILL BE DONE—if it were God's will. Father Kino hoped it was not. He hoped that drawing the slip of paper was an accident and not divine direction. Or perhaps this was God's way to test him, to test his obedience. If Mexico were to be his lot, Eusebio Kino would take it willingly, but he still hoped for China.

The longing of so many years was difficult to give up lightly. God's ways were slow; time would show him the trail he was to follow.

As for the present, to be actually starting somewhere, no matter what the final destination, was exciting. Kino had enthusiasm for all that life brought him; now he let his enthusiasm have full power. He and Father Antonio lost no time in starting their journey.

The plan was for them to go overland to Genoa. There they were to meet other Jesuit missionaries from other parts of Europe. From Genoa the entire party would embark in sailing vessels, down the coast of the Mediterranean Sea, through the Strait of Gibraltar, and on to Cadiz in Spain. From Cadiz, again in a sailing ship, they would cross the wide Atlantic to Vera Cruz, Mexico. Those who were to work in New Spain would go to Mexico City. Those bound for Asia would go to Acapulco, Mexico, from which port they would sail the blue Pacific.

The overland trip from Vera Cruz would be made by muleback. This last caused the two young priests great merriment. It seemed a long distance to go by muleback. In fact, the whole trip seemed a long distance to them. The speed the ships could make would depend on wind and weather, but what would determine the speed of the mules neither of them could even guess.

Yet, if luck were with them, long before the year was completed, Kino thought, he would be saving souls in a foreign land.

The young priest thanked God that at last the work he so wanted to do was so close at hand. He was an eager and impatient man. That he exercised patience at all was the result of long years of discipline. He was a dreamer of big dreams, a worker and a planner, but above all he was dedicated to the Company of Jesus and the God they served.

Young Father Kino always had time for prayer. Now he prayed. He thanked God for this opportunity of serving Him. He asked Saint Francis to pray for the success of his work, and to make it in China, if God so willed.

The two young priests left Ottingen, traveling by coach and four. At this time in Upper Germany the coach was a common carrier, as well as a luxury for royalty. Anyone who had the money for fare could go by coach. Although coach bodies were still without springs, they were suspended from leather straps. This made riding in them somewhat more comfortable than when they had been suspended from four posts. But no amount of discomfort could have saddened the hearts of the two young missionaries. Their joy could not be lessened. They had begun their journey. The thought that this journey might end for either of them with a martyr's crown in heaven did not dismay them. During their school days each mail had brought word of some Jesuit who had gone the martyr's road. All over the world each Jesuit missionary knew that such an end might be his. He not only accepted this, he embraced it.

The trip from Ottingen to Trent was in exact reverse to the one made many years before by the boy, Eusebio. But this time it was more enjoyable. This time Father Kino could look backward with satisfaction at what he had accomplished. He could look forward with serenity because now his way was clearly marked.

So the two young priests left Ottingen one nippy March morning, riding across the plains of Upper Germany. Their first stop was at Munich. Perhaps Father Kino gave a thought to what his life might have been had he accepted the offered professorship at Munich University. But if he did give thought, it was without regret. The two Fathers stayed six days in Munich packing, unpacking, repacking the things they would need to take with them. This done, they were on their way by coach again—to Innsbruck this time, stopping overnight at the college in Hall.

Hall was dear to Father Kino's heart. Here good health had been given back to him; here he had made his vow to enter the Jesuit order. Later he had come to Hall as an inexperienced, eager teacher brimming over with ideas to give to the boys he taught.

When Father Kino and Father Antonio arrived at the college, the teachers and students welcomed them. Everyone wanted to know their plans, to the smallest detail. The priests who hoped for foreign missions wished that they, too, might be taking this trip. Prayers were said that night, and Mass was offered the next morning, for the two missionaries.

Father Kino found it difficult to say good-by. It was a little sad to realize that perhaps he might not pass this way nor see these friends again. But he was young; the grief of parting was softened by the expectancy of what was to come.

Soon after leaving Innsbruck, the two reached the Brenner highroad. Today, as when first Eusebio Kino had traveled it, traffic was heavy with the milling crowds. Now, however, instead of seeing a crowd of people, Father Kino could put each man in the place that fitted him. His gaze, from the lurching coach window, sorted out the travelers. They were monks, merchants and students; they were minstrels, jugglers and craftsmen; they were pilgrims and beggars. Alone and together they went their way along the Brenner highroad.

The highroad was dotted with inns. They had always been there, but Father Kino seemed more aware of them today. They were much the same: two- or three-storied buildings with low, wide-spreading eaves, their huge doorways always arched, sometimes with marble. Inside each archway was a high vaulted hall floored with stone. This hall gave entrance into kitchens, storerooms, wine cellars and eating-rooms for the common people. At the end of the hall the wide stone stairway led to the second floor and the dining room for gentle folks where the priests were welcomed.

Although all of the inns were much the same, each night Father Kino greeted a new one with new delight. He especially loved the innyards so bursting with noise and confusion. He was never too weary to walk about, looking at the horses, pack trains, carts, road wagons, coaches and people. He had a question and a word for everyone. He was a perfect traveler, seeing everything there was to see with curiosity and interest and pleasure. He learned the what and the why and the how of everything he saw.

Not far from the Pass were the Brenner Baths, warm mineral springs which, since ancient times, had been open for the use of all travelers. Beggars in particular were welcome. Everyone too poor to pay was allowed a free bath and was given a small piece of money to buy his food and free salt to make it tasty. Father Kino walked among these people, talking with them and giving them his blessing.

After the Baths came Brenner Pass. Once through it, the two priests were in the Vol di Non.

The young Father Kino looked everywhere at once. There were the mountain peaks, brooding and waiting. There was the River Noce, noisy and swift-flowing. Then soon, much sooner than it had taken to walk it, was the home village. There, thanks be to God, was the village of Segno.

There is nothing more precious to a Tyrol village than to give a son to the service of

God. When the village priest or the schoolmaster tells a father he has a son who bears the sign of a chosen one, there is great rejoicing. His parents, his family, his neighbors have a special part and a special pride in this divine blessing. No sacrifice is too great for any of them to make. They send him away to be taught, to be trained, to be accepted for the priesthood. They pray for his ordination.

When the time for his returning comes, whether as pastor or visitor, there is great preparation for celebration and festival.

This was true with Father Eusebio Francisco Kino. He had sent word that he, the boy from Segno, was going as a missionary to a foreign land. But first he would come back to Segno, to say Mass in the village church, to give his blessing to his village people.

His village people had received the word and they had made ready to receive him. At the village edge the two priests climbed from the coach and waited for the long procession to approach them. Although the villagers were dressed in their gayest costumes, it was a serious moment. Their boy had come home a priest, a man of God. They loved him with reverence. They honored him with pride.

At the head of the procession walked the

village priest. Father Arnoldus had years ago gone to God, but he had left one to shepherd his flock and bring them home to the pastures of heaven. Behind the priest walked the village band, the pride of Segno. Following the zither players and the carolers were Eusebio's sisters, their husbands and families. Then the rest of the townspeople came: young, middle-aged and old.

Eusebio's parents were not there, nor were his godparents. They, like Father Arnoldus, had walked the road to eternity. Father Eusebio missed them. With the village pastor, the young priests walked to Eusebio's oldest sister's home, where they refreshed themselves. Then, again in procession, they went to the church for the evening Angelus and Vespers.

Inside and outside, the church was hung with garlands. How many times, as a boy, Eusebio had hung garlands for a feast day! Today they had been hung for him. His people had garlanded the church for him. Blessing them, his eyes were full of tears.

After Vespers there was feasting and merrymaking until the midnight bell was sounded. Almost at once the little village, unused to late hours and feasting, went to sleep. But Father Eusebio did not sleep. He could not.

Dawn came and morning Angelus. As he stood by the church door, the young priest could see the wayside shrine on the river road. He remembered the boy who had knelt there so many years ago. Slowly he walked into the church.

The Mass began, his Mass, Father Eusebio Kino's Mass in the church of his boyhood. Father Antonio assisted him, and all the people knelt in adoration as the Segno boy consecrated the Bread and the Wine, the Body and the Blood of Christ the Savior.

Unlike Hall, here in Segno, Father Eusebio's going to the New World seemed of small importance to the people. To them the important thing—the beautiful, glorious thing—was that their Eusebio Kino had become a priest. His hands were holy because they were empowered to break the Bread and to bless the Wine. That he was going to the New World was less important to them.

As for Father Eusebio Kino, when it was time to go, the going was not as hard as he had feared it might be. His priest, his parents, his godparents were gone. He missed them and the life that once had been his, although he did not want to return to it. It was sweet in memory. He was content to have it so. The other time had been truly his final farewell; this was repetition.

The ride to Trent was uneventful. The young priests were silent and thoughtful, their minds and hearts filled with prayer. To Father Kino, Trent looked much the same as when he had gone to school there. In a city as old as Trent, change is not measured by decades. He thought it looked less elegant than he remembered it, but perhaps his tastes had grown with his experiences. He did not know. He knew only that he was glad when Trent was left behind and Milan lay in front of them.

From Trent to Milan, the route was unfamiliar. Father Kino's lively curiosity interested him in everything he saw along the way. There was never anything too unimportant to escape his quick notice and simple pleasure.

Milan lay in the middle of the rich and fertile Lombard plain on the little river of Olona. The patchwork fields around the city were vivid with new green. The countryside looked like a lovely garden outlined in Lombardy poplar and mulberry trees. The entire plain was dotted with small villages like wild flowers blooming in a pasture land.

The city of Milan was large and rich and cultured. Followers of all the arts were drawn there like flies to honey. The Lombard school of sculpture was the most renowned in the world at that time. Moreover, the city was rich in art galleries that held some of the finest pictures in Europe.

Only two other churches, Saint Peter's in Rome and the Cathedral of Seville, were larger than the Cathedral of Milan. Father Kino was impressed with its beauty and its size. The boy from Segno was seeing wondrous things. He was amazed by them, but not so amazed that he could tarry for a second sight. There was still the distance from Milan to Genoa which must be covered quickly. The two Jesuits said good-by to Milan and hurried onward. They could not wait. It was the second of May when they arrived at Genoa. The first thing Father Kino saw was the harbor and, riding at anchor, the wooden sailing vessels with their tall graceful masts.

Genoa was the town where Christopher Columbus had been born. This was the harbor the boy Columbus had known. Father Kino looked at the harbor now and thanked God for their safe arrival. He asked Francis Xavier to pray for their quick departure.

Jesuits of Genoa met the two missionaries from Upper Germany and took them to their college to await the arrival of the others who were to join them. Father Kino and Father Antonio had been the first to come.

Before long, seventeen other Jesuits, bound for missions to foreign lands, arrived, all of them impatient to get started to Cadiz. It was now well into May, and the Spanish royal fleet, on which they had been promised passage, was to sail sometime in July. There was no time to spare if they were to get to Cadiz in time to sail with it.

Sea travel, as well as being dangerous, was uncertain. Arrival at any particular place at a set time was uncertain. Embarkation from port was uncertain. Getting passage on a ship was the most uncertain of all. There were no common-carrier ships, no fixed routes of travel, and no exact schedules.

Fleets were made up of ships sponsored by royal governments or by merchants of a country. Merchant ships were private property. Their purpose was to take merchandise to trade and to barter. They put in at ports suited for their purposes and sailed at times that were best for the merchants who owned them. Besides the crew, they had to carry soldiers for the protection of their merchandise, so there was little room to spare for ordinary passengers.

Even the royal fleets sailed only from time to time. When at last the missionaries arrived at Genoa, they learned that there was no royal fleet sailing from that port, nor was there likelihood of any for some time to come. The Jesuits therefore tried to get passage on some merchant ship, but without success. Time passed. Their impatience turned to worry.

It was June before the nineteen Jesuits succeeded in obtaining passage on the flagship *Capitana*, which was being accompanied by a smaller vessel. Its captain, Francisco Columbus, was a descendant of Christopher, and this seemed a favorable omen. The Jesuit Fathers from the college in Genoa took their guests down to the harbor, with good-bys and good wishes for a safe journey. The eager young missionaries were rowed out to the flagship. Nothing could stop them now. They had only to sail along the coast, go through the strait at the Rock, and on to Cadiz. Father Kino was a happy man.

He was pleased with everything about the ship. What he did not know, he set about finding out. He counted the passengers; with sailors, soldiers and Jesuits, there were more than two hundred. He measured the ship. He recorded everything that he saw and heard and thought about.

The first day at sea everything went well, but on the second a storm blew up. Most of the Jesuits were seasick; not the boy from Segno. He wrote in his diary that he was only a little sick and had recovered shortly. Heavy sea or not, he was a good traveler.

Then came a time of calm when the travelers wondered if they would reach Cadiz in time to sail with the royal fleet, but no amount of worry would make the wind blow, and without wind a sailing vessel is a thing without movement. But there came a dawn when the wind blew again, the sails swelled and the ships gained speed. Father Kino was jubilant.

On shipboard there were Masses and Vespers and the Angelus, sermons and the Sacraments. Hardened sailors and soldiers who had not bent a knee for years now knelt and prayed.

At length the travelers reached Alicante, a Spanish seaport. Everything had delayed them. As Father Kino looked at the flat-roofed city, the castle, and the lighthouse, he wished they need not put in here at all. He wished they would keep on going, but Captain Francisco Columbus had other plans. His ships and passengers were to stay in port for more than a week.

The Spanish Jesuits of Alicante came out to meet the new arrivals. All the townspeople, all the priests and church dignitaries welcomed the missionaries. It was a gay occasion and they made the most of it.

Now that he was here and had to stay, Father Kino set out to see everything there was to see. This was the first time he had been in a Spanish town and these were the first Spaniards he had known. He enjoyed the city and the people.

On the night of the arrival of the Jesuits, there was a grand church procession through the streets of the town. Saint Veronica's Veil was being carried from the shrine where it was kept to the cathedral as the people prayed to her to protect the city from the plague, which was raging all through Europe. It was a common sight to see house doors marked with a crimson cross above the words, "God have mercy on their souls." To the passer-by this meant that death waited behind the cross-marked door.

Father Kino watched the procession from the balcony of the Jesuit college. Then he and his companions went to the cathedral to kiss the sacred veil. It was a never-to-be-forgotten experience. To see the tortured face of Christ imprinted so perfectly, so delicately on the veil the saint had carried, to touch it, to kiss it, filled the young priest with an inflamed desire to follow in the footsteps of the tortured Christ. Silently he renewed his vows. Before leaving Alicante, Father Kino said Mass one morning in the cathedral where the veil had been placed. Many times the memory was to confort and encourage him on the lonely trails he followed.

After a week had passed, Captain Francisco Columbus was ready to sail again. The townspeople, the church people—everybody—came down to the harbor to say farewell. It was a happy occasion for the people of Alicante because they were a happy people, and for them every occasion was a gay one. It was happy for the young missionaries because they were on their way again.

The ships kept to a slow and steady speed, and at last Gibraltar was sighted. Father Kino looked in delight at the Rock and the outlines of the old Moorish castle near by. So often he had despaired of seeing it, but now, thanks be to Saint Francis, the great Rock loomed above him, dark, brooding, gigantic. Then it was lost in night mist.

At the mouth of the strait, the pilot got off course. All night the two boats sailed in the wrong direction. At dawn the mistake was discovered and the course was righted, but once again precious time had been lost. In the late afternoon, Father Kino sighted the harbor of Cadiz. Gracefully, proudly the flagship and the smaller vessel sailed toward it into the setting sun.

The Jesuits stood together at the rail—and then, between themselves and the sunset rays, they sighted a group of vessels. Father Kino counted forty-four of them sailing over the darkening horizon. The Jesuits stood watching the royal Spanish ships sail away to the Indies. They had missed the departure hour.

Chapter 4

IT TOOK THE SAILING VESSELS four days to get inside the harbor of Cadiz. First, the wind was so strong that twice the flagship's sails were torn. Later, because the plague was raging within the city, the health officials were slow to give Captain Columbus permission to land. But at last the weather calmed, the necessary papers were signed, and the Jesuits were landed in Cadiz.

Though their hearts were heavy that the royal fleet had not waited for them, they spent no time in regret. Years of discipline had trained them to accept that which had to be accepted.

In a week, having left Cadiz, they were housed in the Jesuit college in Seville where they would wait for a vessel to take them across the Atlantic. They would take the first ship, royal or merchant, that they could get passage on. Presently a trade vessel bound for Africa went by. It had space enough for the missionaries, but they refused the chance, for the trade ship would carry slaves as cargo. They would not go on a slave ship. From time to time there were other ships that could take them, but the fare demanded for passage was too expensive.

The faith of the Fathers kept them serene. God would tend their needs in His good time. So they waited and worked and prayed while they waited. It was a kind of second novitiate, strengthening their patience, toughening their endurance.

Father Kino mastered the Spanish language while he waited. He made a sundial for one of his Jesuit friends. He helped the others make many things that would be useful to them in their mission work. He kept his diary up to date. He visited the Cathedral of Seville many times.

As always, everything the young priest saw was of interest to him. He wrote about everything: the amazing number of monks and monasteries of different religious orders, of the bull fights which the Church objected to, the poverty he saw in certain parts of the city which so saddened him.

Although Seville was a Spanish city, there were many Dutch and French people living there. The control of buying, selling and making things was in their hands. Father Kino was interested in this and recorded it in his diary. This habit of seeing everything and writing about it never left him. Years later he was doing the same careful, exact recording of what he saw. Centuries later this material became a thoughtful and truthful history of his time and place.

But even to Father Kino the two years of waiting in Seville seemed an eternity. By this time the missionary band had grown to twenty-three—twenty-three young, eager, earnest, dedicated men who tried to wait patiently for God to make it possible for them to do His work.

At last their prayers were answered. They were able to get passage on the *Nazareno*. What a day of thankfulness this was! What a time of rejoicing! The missionaries hurried back to Cadiz, taking with them all the good and useful things they had made in Seville. It seemed as if this might have been the purpose of their two years of waiting. Perhaps they had been given this chance to make those things which would enrich their labors in foreign lands.

When they arrived in Cadiz, the Fathers learned that the *Nazareno* was one of the ships of a large West Indian fleet on its way to Mexico. Though they had hurried to get back to Cadiz, it was not until three months later that the fleet made ready to sail. The Jesuits boarded the *Nazareno*, and good-bys, which had now become habit, were said once more.

Almost immediately after they set sail, the pilot of the *Nazareno* ran the ship on a sand bar. Wind drove it against a rock, and water poured into the damaged vessel. The Captain ordered that all cargo be thrown overboard. For the missionaries this meant the loss of everything they owned, all their possessions. They watched their work of two years go down into an angry sea. But even the lightening of the vessel did not help.

The Jesuits were put in a launch and returned to Cadiz. There they went about all night, begging passage on the other ships that made up the fleet. Some ships could find a place for one or two, and by dawn places for eleven missionaries had been found. The other twelve would need to wait again. Father Eusebio Francisco Kino was among the twelve. Three years had passed since the day he had drawn the fateful slip of paper.

When all hope was gone of getting passage on the West Indian fleet, ten of the Fathers returned to Seville. Father Kino and one other were left to work and wait and pray in Cadiz, where the plague was raging. Death walked the streets both day and night. It was a sad and desolate city, a sad and desolate time. Days on earth seemed so short, Father Kino thought. He had but one desire—to spend these days bringing unbelieving souls to God—but his days seemed to be passing without that goal being realized.

Eusebio Kino had not been born a saint. He had been born a man—an eager, impatient man. He was a dreamer, but not a dreamer content with dreams. He wanted his dreams to come true. That his dreams were for God's glory made him but more restless and more determined. They filled him with greater fury to realize them.

He began to doubt. Perhaps the slip of

paper which said, "Mexico," had not been intended as his destiny. Perhaps there was mission work for him in China after all. This last thought rekindled the flame of his desire to go to the Orient. He prayed with renewed vigor. Again he wrote letters to Jesuits who were being sent to China, asking them to request his services if they needed him. Again he wrote to the Father General in Rome.

Another priest who was being sent to the Orient gave Father Kino new hope by telling him about the Duchess of Aviero y Arco. She was a Spanish noblewoman of great wealth and piety, known far and wide for her good works. Missionary priests all over the world wrote to her for help. They called her the Mother of Missions. She shared her wealth freely, and also had great influence at the court of Madrid and with Church dignitaries. Father Kino wrote to the Duchess about his plight and asked her help.

While he waited an answer from Rome and help from the Duchess, Father Kino was not idle. He became interested in a comet that appeared each evening in the sky over Cadiz. It was known as Heaven's Chariot, was of unusual brilliancy, and was said to appear every five hundred years. In his diary, the priest noted its exact position in the sky each evening. The record stands to this day. He also wrote that the comet was a bad omen, but perhaps his thoughts during those days were dark ones.

Father Kino received no answer from Rome, but the Duchess wrote him kindly and hopeful letters and sent him small gifts such as little crosses to use when he went to his mission. She was a comfort in this time of waiting, but she could not help him get permission to be sent to the Orient.

His destiny seemed to have been written on the slip of paper.

In January, 1681, the band of twelve Jesuits joined a fleet bound for Panama. They would go in a dispatch boat which would sail by way of Puerto Rico to Vera Cruz in Mexico. The missionaries who had been waiting in Seville again hurried to Cadiz. Because of the quarantine for plague, they could not enter the city, but they had no reason to do so, for to them Cadiz was merely a place to leave from. They were content to wait at the harbor for Father Kino and his companion, who lost no time in joining them.

It was a good reunion, and there were many things to talk about, but they lost no time in talking until their band was safely out to sea.

And now at last the sailing across the wide Atlantic, so long hoped and prayed for, became reality.

The long journey was a rough one. The dispatch boat was tossed about by the raging wind. Though Father Kino was a good sailor, poor Father Antonio was seasick most of the time. Yet it was Father Antonio who had been selected for the much longer voyage to China. Father Kino wondered about this. It seemed easier to accept than to try to understand the ways of God. He prayed for patience. He prayed for China, too, but always he said, "Thy will, not mine."

On the first of May they landed at Vera Cruz, bringing to end a sea journey of ninety-six days.

Father Kino was filled with joy. Everything he saw seemed beautiful and wonderful. Sailing into the harbor, he looked at the snowy cone of Mont Orizaba rising eighteen thousand feet above the sea. It was so different from the Alps of Segno, yet momentarily it brought the Vol di Non into memory. The wave-splashed coastland was vivid green with plants and swaying palm trees, spotted with all kinds of unfamiliar flowers in brilliant colors. The rainy season was beginning and the hot ground steamed from recent showers. The air was heavy with sea smell and the smell of damp earth and lush plant growth. Father Kino sniffed with pleasure and with happy expectation of what was to come.

Though Vera Cruz was the most important port in Mexico, it was neither large nor elegant. The buildings were low, most of them flat-roofed, and the streets were straight. The churches were very grand, however, and there were many monastaries belonging to different Orders.

The missionaries were met by two Jesuits and taken to their college, where they met two others who had come from Mexico City to meet them and escort them back. They set out in a week, traveling by muleback, with pack burros to carry their luggage. Father Kino was delighted. He was traveling as Saint Francis would have traveled had he been with them.

The mule train followed the narrow old trail of Cortez. The first part of the journey was level enough. It lay across the flat, coastal plain —a hot, steamy jungle stretch. *Tierra Caliente* it was called, the Hot Land. As they jogged along, sweat filled Father Kino's eyes and ran in streams down his body. Trees, vines, ferns, flowers crowded the sides of the trail. Insects filled the air with angry buzzing sounds.

Now and then in the cleared places there were clusters of houses unlike any Father Kino had seen before, at least at close distance. They were built of bamboo and wild, tough grass, their roofs steep and thatched, some with palm fronds or wild grass bunches tied together. All the houses were green and blended perfectly into their jungle setting, to become a part of the natural background. All of the building materials were close at hand. Nothing needed to be traded for nor brought in from a distance. They could be had for the cutting.

Soon the mule train had crossed the coastal plain and begun to climb through the foothills. They climbed slowly but steadily from sea level to three, four thousand feet. As they climbed, the air changed. It became lighter, cooler. The riders were now in *Tierra Templada*, the Temperate Land. The daily rain came down as it had in *Tierra Caliente*, not steaming and soft, but sharp and cool.

The houses also changed and became more like small villages than family group shelters. The materials used had changed, too. The houses of the Temperate Land were of sun-dried adobe bricks, well made to give shelter from wind and storm, sun and rain. They were red-brown, as the hills and the soil were red-brown. The roofs were not as steep as those in the Hot Land and were made of red tile from the clay near by and baked in the village kiln.

The stops made along the way were short ones, only for needed rest or the getting together of needed supplies. But Father Kino made the most of each short stop. He saw; he learned; he remembered. This was his way.

Before many days the foothill country of temperate climate also was left behind. The narrow trails became steep and dangerous. The Jesuits on their mules climbed steadily to six, seven thousand feet. The rains which came down each day were more severe. Often there was hail, and the high peaks were snow-covered. There seemed to be more Indian villages along the trail. They, too, climbed up the mountain slopes, as far as eye could see, often as high as the tree line. The houses of these villages were of stone, sometimes of beautifully cut stone, but inside they were like the houses of the Hot and Temperate Lands: one room, a cooking place, hammocks or woven sleeping mats, clay ollas, and brightly painted wooden bowls.

So the weeks went by, as day by day they

went jogging along the trails, stopping in settlements of some kind as darkness overtook them. The priests were welcomed wherever they stopped. Most of the Indians along the way had only a vague idea of who the blackrobes were or where they were going. They neither knew nor cared. These men were strangers, travelers. This was enough. They shared what they had with them.

As the missionaries neared Puebla, City of the Angels, Father Kino's excitement mounted. Puebla was not far from Mexico City; he was nearing another goal. A day's journey out from Puebla, the priests were met by the Father Provincial from Mexico City who had come with several other priests, in coaches, to welcome the missionaries. The newly-arriving Jesuits must enter the City of the Angels in style befitting their importance as priests of God.

The coaches were not much more comfortable than the jogging mules had been, but the welcome was warm. The weary priests responded to their brothers' welcome. The ride into the city was gay with conversation, with questions and answers, with bits of information given and received.

As the coaches lurched over the cobblestone road, the great mountain Popo looked down at the long line of carriages and mules and pack burros. Smoke curled and belched from its crater top. Its snow-covered slopes were dazzling white in the rain-filled sunlight. The Indians believed, the Mexican Jesuits told the new arrivals, that Popo was the final resting place for all their rulers who had been wicked, and the smoke rising from its cone was proof that they were being punished. The Indians also said that no man could climb their mountain and live. Father Kino remembered from his reading that one of the men with Cortez had climbed it—and lived. But he did not say this. He was listening, not talking.

A further welcome waited the travelers at the gates of the Jesuit college. The entire staff —about forty priests—was crowded around the gates, eager to welcome their visitors and show them their church. The church was a surprise and a delight to Father Kino, for it was more beautiful and more gold-filled than any he had seen in Europe.

Next morning, on the road again, Father Kino's gladness of heart grew within him. Each league he traveled brought him much nearer to the realization of his work for God. The narrow road was little better than a cattle trail. It climbed and wound and curved back upon itself, twisting higher into the mountains. There was always a place to stay at night, always a welcome.

Father Kino was interested in the people he met by the trail-side: Indians, Mexican, Spanish—three separate and distinct groups in folkways, in beliefs, and in living standards. But all of them welcomed the travelers, gave them what they had, and made them feel at home.

Quite often the pack train spent the night at some hacienda. There were hundreds of them in those days in that part of the country. Some belonged to different religious Orders, who used them as supply centers for their missions. More of them belonged to wealthy Spanish haciendados who had received their land as royal grants from Spanish kings.

An hacienda was a complete little world within itself. Probably the only thing it did not raise, grow or make for its own needs was salt, and sometimes even this was available to haciendas located near salt beds. Haciendas gave training, work, home, food and a way of life to thousands of Indians and mixed bloods. Every hacienda had its farm workers, herders and shepherds, its masons, smiths and carpenters, its potters, weavers and house servants. Every hacienda had its store and its church.

Many had their own jewelry-makers and most of them had a priest or a priest-visitor.

Father Kino went into every corral and corner of every hacienda where they spent the night. He saw the fields and the pastures, the gardens and the orchards. He saw the horse herds, and cattle and sheep and swine. He went into the storerooms, the granary and the mill. He visited the servants' quarters and the workrooms. He was the honored guest in the big house where the haciendado and his family lived.

Eusebio Kino recalled his father's farm in the Vol di Non. It, too, had been a place where the people raised and grew or made most of the things they needed. But it had been a village. There had been families and heads of families. The village had prospered only as the families had cooperated and had given to it that which each family thought right. The hacienda was not a village made up of many independent families, but a kind of one-family organization. There was only one head: the owner, the haciendado. He gave the orders, the directions, the training. The people in his hacienda were his children. He taught them the things they needed to know.

The Italian priest from the Alps, where

every man was his own master, looked at this new organization where men were children. This system seemed successful here in this new, raw land where many were indeed children in the ways of those who had conquered them. Father Kino looked and asked questions and was thoughtful. He tucked away in a corner of his mind each bit of information he gathered. He would remember it, and if need arose he would use it.

It was June by the time the Jesuit party crossed the valley of the Anahuac to enter the ancient, splendid capital city of the Aztecs, now the capital of Mexico. In the old days, three lakes had encircled the city. It could be entered only by three stone causeways which were connected by drawbridges. In some places these causeways were so wide that Cortez horsemen rode proudly twelve abreast along their time-worn pavements.

This day in June, the pack train of the Jesuit missionary Fathers trotted along the ancient causeway into the city. They rode single file but no less proudly than the horsemen of an earlier time. They, too, carried the royal banner of Spain and the holy Cross of Christianity. The long way of many leagues and many years from Genoa to Mexico now lay behind them.

Soon their band, who had come together in Genoa, would be scattered through the mission fields of the world. Some of them would gain the martyr's crown. The rest would walk the lonely trails of foreign lands until God in His mercy called them to their reward.

Father Kino thought these things as he jogged along the ancient causeway. He did not think of Segno nor Trent, of Innsbruck nor Ingolstadt. He did not think of the weary years of waiting in Seville and Cadiz. It was not like him to let his thoughts run backward. Rather they forged ahead. His mind raced with them, with dreams abuilding. Smartly, proudly he urged his mule along the way. Mexico City lay just beyond the turn.

Chapter 5

FATHER KINO was surprised at the size of Mexico City. There were sixty thousand houses or more where the *ricos* lived in style and the poor existed. He was interested in the kinds of houses they lived in. It took little time for the curious young missionary to learn that the houses of the *ricos* were built of lava rock and those belonging to the poor of sun-dried brick.

In all parts of the city the public plazas and the patio gardens were beautiful. Rich and poor alike enjoyed the flowers and the plants of the fertile land. For Father Kino this was especially delightful. The European cities he had known had been old and formal and patterned. The fresh new beauty of Mexico seemed so full of hope and promise it was a joy to behold.

Although the city was rich in natural beauty, it also had been adorned by man. The public buildings were elaborate and elegant. The Colonial Palace was large enough to house the seat of government, an armory, the city granary, a zoo and an aviary.

The magnificence of the many churches filled the European priests with awe. They had seen nothing like them in Europe. Here the entire church walls were covered with gold-leaf and hung with paintings by European masters. Many of the church vessels were of gold. In the cathedral the altar and the candlesticks were of solid silver. These were the worldly treasures of the New World; surely the souls that could be saved here would be the priceless Treasures of heaven. Father Kino looked and admired and was thoughtful.

There was a gaiety and informality here that had not been known in Europe. The cathedral was the center of the life of the city—of religious life, as would be expected, but also of government and social life. Before the cathedral every evening the *ricos* promenaded. Slowly, sedately the beautiful young women circled the plaza before the cathedral doors. In the opposite direction the young *rico* men circled. Sitting on the plaza benches, the old watched everyone and everything that happened.

All through the hours of the day, huddled against the massive church walls, the beggars of the city begged their bread. The peddlers called their wares and sold to the *ricos* and the poor alike. Through the crowd, the sounds, the sights, the movements of the city, the Jesuits walked by twos and threes, mingling with the people, getting to know them and their city.

After evening Angelus, the city crier called the news of the day. Shipwreck or pirate attack at sea, earthquake or volcano eruption were called out to the people that they might know the news of the world. Just before the arrival of Father Kino and his companions in Mexico, the Pueblo rebellion had taken place in New Mexico. Here in the Cathedral of Mexico City there had been an elaborate funeral for the twenty-one Franciscans who had been killed during that bloody time. Every evening the crier gave added news of what was happening in the country to the north.

The European missionaries were eager for

every bit of information they could get. Some of them would go into or at least near the Pueblo country. Father Kino wondered where he would be sent. He wondered what kind of people he would be living with and serving. As always, he fretted at delay. All he really wanted was work, a mule to ride, and souls to save.

For the time being, this was not to happen. Father Kino's fame as a European scholar had preceded him to Mexico. At once he was taken into the society of the scholars of the city. At this time the Royal University of Mexico was over a hundred years old. Its faculty was made up of learned professors, many of them having been born in Mexico. The New World was proud of its learning and fearful that the Old World considered itself more learned. Father Kino was welcomed into this circle. His new friends were eager to learn from him and to show him what they knew.

University life was interesting to Father Kino. As with everything else, he accepted it with enthusiasm. He became particularly interested in the old Mayan and Aztec cultures. He studied what these ancient peoples had accomplished in weaving, pottery-making and stone-carving. He was amazed at their achievements.

Yet they had not been a Christian people, nor were their descendants Christian. Here would be a fertile field, the eager priest thought, for some missionary who would plant the seed and harvest it in His name.

Father Kino studied the ancient Mayan calendar. He was surprised that these unlettered people had developed a calendar which was more exact than any that had been developed in Europe. It was hard to believe, but facts were facts.

Their culture here in Mexico was in many ways as rich as Chinese culture. These people were surely as worthy of Christianity as were the unbelievers of the Orient. Yet it was difficult to give up a dream of so many years. It was difficult to substitute a strange people for those whom one had known about since early boyhood.

He still wanted to go to China, Father Kino decided. He wanted to do God's will, but that will had not yet been shown clearly to him. He began to write letters again. He wrote to one of his Jesuit friends who was gathering together missionaries for the Orient. Father Kino begged for a place with his friend's band. The answer came promptly. Father Kino was wanted. They would be honored to have him as one of their number. They would ask permission of Rome.

Father Kino wrote again to the Duchess. Nothing had been decided, he told her. Perhaps, after all, there was a chance that he might be sent to China. He was saying a weekly Mass at the Shrine of the Virgin of Guadalupe at the edge of the city for this intention. Since Our Lady of Guadalupe was the Duchess's patroness, he added, perhaps she would add her prayers to his.

The weeks became months. The months passed by. Rome did not give its permission that Father Kino be sent to China. The Duchess seemed powerless to help him. At last part of his prayer was answered. An expedition was being prepared to go to California. It was causing great interest and excitement in Spain and in Mexico. Explorers, soldiers, sailors, and workmen were being recruited. There was also need for two priests to accompany the expedition.

The man who volunteered to lead the party had chosen a Jesuit friend as one of the priests who were to go with them. The Viceroy was to select the other one, and he was slow in his selection. A responsible man was needed. In his mind the Viceroy listed the qualifications needed by the priest he would send. He must be dedicated to his calling. Above all else, he must have the welfare of the Indians at heart. He must teach them the Word of God and the ways of the men who had come to colonize their land. He must teach them not to harm the strangers who would henceforth live among them. Above all, he must see that the Indians were treated with kindness and justice. They were to be Christianized, not enslaved. He must be a scholar as well, for he would need to be historian and explorer as well as spiritual director. The Viceroy took his time, but at last he made his selection. He chose Father Eusebio Francisco Kino.

Father Kino was to have charge of the spiritual welfare of the members of the expedition and the Indians whom they would meet and Christianize. He also was to be the Royal Historian, the Royal Astronomer, the Royal Surveyor and the Royal Mapmaker of the party.

God's will had been made known to Father Kino. He was never to go to China. If he grieved, there was no sign of it.

At once he began making ready for his work. He borrowed maps of the Island of California and books about it, though there were very few. He studied, thought, planned, wrote letters. He wrote to the Duchess, asking her for any help she could give him and for her prayers. He promised that he would remember her patroness, Our Lady of Guadalupe, in the new land. Ending his letter, he wrote, "So may the Holy Will be done of Him who always knows what is best." And he added, "And I confess I go with great pleasure."

It was October 1681.

While Father Kino had been waiting in Cadiz for passage to the New World, events were taking place in Mexico that were to be important to him. These events were to determine, guide and shape his life and work in the New World. Yet he knew nothing of them, suspected nothing. Nor was his name brought into their planning. Thus it is that God brings people and events together in His own good time and that He shows His way only when the time is right for showing it.

In 1679, while Father Kino was still in Cadiz, the royal government of Spain decided to expand its New World holdings by sending an expedition to take possession of and explore the Island of California. If it was to be practical, the expedition would colonize the island and Christianize the Indians living there.

To all ports, villages and towns of Mexico

messengers were sent to tell of the royal decision. Church bells rang in all the plazas. People gathered in front of the churches to hear their town criers give them this news. There was great excitement throughout the country. Such an expedition should bring new treasures for the royal Spanish chest and new souls for God's glory. It also would bring opportunities for adventure for those seeking adventure, and work for those who wanted work.

The expedition would need seamen and soldiers, carpenters and caulkers, gunsmiths, common laborers, and two priests. It would need equipment to be imported from Spain and supplies to be gathered together in Mexico. It would need horses and mules, horsemen and pack trains and sailing ships.

The first need was for a man who could lead such a large and important expedition. Don Isidro Atondo, a Spaniard, offered his services to the Spanish King. Don Isidro, an able man, had been a soldier and a seaman and as both had proven his ability and his courage. He had been a successful governor of Sinaloa and Sonora. He knew how to command; he was respected by all who knew him. In every way Don Isidro seemed to be the man the Spanish government was seeking. They accepted his offer and gave him complete authority and responsibility for the expedition.

His contract was for five years. At least two of these years must be spent in preparation for the undertaking, and at least one year must be spent actually living in California. Don Isidro agreed to take with him Christianized Indians from Sinaloa who would be used as servants and would also be good examples for the untamed Indians of California.

As soon as the contract was signed, Don Isidro began preparatory work. His first task was to build frigates and launches for the voyage. These ships also would be used to go back and forth from California to the mainland for necessary communication and supplies. Later they would be used to transport colonists to the new possessions.

Don Isidro chose the small pueblo of Nio on the Sinaloa River to be his ship-building base. Nio was a peaceful, sleepy town which had been Christianized for almost a hundred years, and in almost all of this time nothing had happened to disturb its slumber. But much was happening now. The town wakened: it gained new life, new people, new ways as ship-building activities began. Although ship-building was a new occupation for Nio, it was not a new occupation for other parts of the Pacific coast. Since the time of Balboa many of the ships that had explored the western coastline had been built in some quiet harbor of the blue Pacific. So Nio boomed and was noisy and busy and money flowed through the dusty streets.

When Father Kino received word that he was to join the expedition, he made haste to get to Nio, leaving Mexico City in October of 1681 to go muleback across the continent. By November he had reached Guadalajara. From there he rode on to Nio.

For several months he seemed to be everywhere at once. He made many trips from Nio to Guadalajara to get necessary papers for his missionary duties in the expedition. There were delays and letters and visits and further delays. Father Kino had no intention of getting this far and having trouble because he did not have the correct papers. He wrote as many letters and made as many trips and paid as many visits as were necessary to get the papers signed and sealed.

Besides jogging to and fro on muleback from Nio to Guadalajara, Father Kino made visits to many of the other towns and ports on the western coast. His days were full of business, and he saw to each task personally.

The port of Chacalo had been selected as shipping point for the expedition. It was an old port which Coronado had used a hundred and forty years before, when he set sail from there to conquer the seven cities of Cibola. Atondo used it now, and Father Kino and his mule were frequent visitors there.

The Spanish government had given a sum of money for the buying of gifts for the California Indians. These gifts were in charge of the two missionaries of the expedition and were to be distributed by them. They included such things as coarse woolen cloth and colored ribbons, glass beads and knives. Father Kino supervised the purchasing and packing of these gifts. He fingered each one lovingly, dreaming how best it could be used to coax a wild Indian near enough to listen to the teachings of Christ.

The young priest never seemed to tire. His enthusiasm never lacked its spark. Each new day he was able to find some additional task that needed his immediate attention. If there was ever thought of China, no one knew it. That desire belonged to his time of indecision when God's way had not been shown to him.

God's way was clear now. Eusebio Kino followed it with a joyful heart and prayers for a fruitful harvest.

Four years had passed since Don Isidro Atondo had signed his contract to lead the California expedition, but at last his ships were ready—two sturdy frigates, two launches and a balandra. He named his ships the *Almeranta*, the *Capitana* and the *Balandra*. The Jesuit Fathers blessed them. Now he was ready to sail, except for some missing crewmen. He waited a week and then sailed without them. They would follow on the *Balandra*, which would wait for them and sail at a later date.

It was a great day for Nio. The ships were finished, and they were strong and seaworthy. The church bells rang. The people gathered at the river. They pushed the *Almeranta* and the *Capitana* into the water, cheering and shouting, and waved good-by. It had been a good time. They were sorry it was over.

On shipboard the passengers waved back. They were glad to go. Father Kino prayed that Francis Xavier would ask God's blessing on the voyage that lay before them and the work that lay ahead.

Chacalo was but a short distance on the coast down the river from Nio, but it took seven days to get there. It seemed a year to Father Kino. He was impatient to get to the great Island that lay in sight and yet seemed so far away.

Nio had been an exciting and a busy place, but it was calm and quiet compared to Chacalo when the ships anchored in the harbor. Pack trains milled about in great confusion. Royal messengers dashed around on horseback, important with authority. A steady line of sweating men went from the government storehouse to the ships with cannon and fodder, equipment and supplies. Vendors called their wares in a last frantic attempt to sell. Soldiers marched and seamen pushed through the narrow streets.

Father Kino saw that the church vestments and church vessels were safely aboard. He saw that not a single box was missing with his precious gifts for the soon-to-be-converted Indians.

At sunset on March 18th the vessel sailed. Sky and sea were streaked with the gold and crimson colors of the ending day. Behind them in Chacalo the church bell for evening Angelus rang sweet and clear. For a moment's flash Eusebio Francisco Kino, missionary of the Company of Jesus, saw the boy Eusebio on the road to Trent by the River Noce. That had been twenty years ago. Twenty short years of preparation to walk in the footsteps of Christ! How good God had been to him!

For the next five days the ships lay close to shore, there being no wind, no movement of anything, only the still and glassy sea and the still and empty sky. Then there was wind and they sailed again. On April first they anchored across the Gulf in the bay of La Paz and gazed in delight at the lovely land along the shore. Guns were shot and the cannons roared. After Vespers, the drummer boy drummed for attention; the ship crier shouted. When all was quiet, when all were listening, the public scribe read Don Isidro Atondo's Banda. The Banda was direct and to the point. It said clearly what the men could and could not do. The penalty for disobedience was death. Atondo's Banda stated that this was not a trade expedition. It was an expedition for the gathering of souls to God. Their King had spent much gold that they succeed in this.

The men were not to take pearls nor gold nor amber from the Indians. They were not to anger or abuse the Indians. They were not to trade with them. If an Indian in gratitude or friendship gave them gifts, they could keep all but one-fifth. This fifth was for their King.

It was to be put in a chest the King had provided for this purpose. The chest had three keys, and Atondo and two other men were responsible for the keys and the treasures which the chest would contain.

His Banda having been read, Don Isidro Atondo went ashore and selected the site for the camp, in a grove of palm trees beside a spring of water. Mountains rose in the background. Sea waters lapped the shore.

The next day the men landed and went ashore and looked at the site Don Isidro had selected. They liked what they saw and were happy and enthusiastic. On April fifth, with pomp and ceremony, the expedition took formal possession of the land. The men dressed in their best. Atondo wore his uniform, and the Jesuits their vestments. The soldiers marched in military order behind the banner bearer. On one side of the crimson flag was the painted image of Our Lady of Remedia; on the other side was the royal arms of the Kingdom of Spain. A cross was made of a tall palm tree and planted in the sand. Torches were lighted. Guns were fired. The royal banner was waved as three times the shout went skyward, "Long live Carlos Segundos, Monarch of the Spains, our King and Lord."

Atondo took possession of the land in the King's name. The two Jesuit priests took spiritual possession in the name of God. Father Kino blessed the land and the men and the work that lay before them.

It was April 1683.

Chapter 6

HAVING TAKEN POSSESSION of the land in the name of God and King, Father Kino looked around for Indians. Now that he was here, he wanted to start working. It had taken long enough to get here. There was no time to spare if he was to make up for the long years he had waited in Seville and Cadiz. He had come to give the Word of God to the Indians and he was ready to begin.

There were no Indians. All day Father Kino

waited for them, but none came. So he went looking for them. He found tracks at the spring where they had come for water. He found more tracks in the wooded land near by, where they had come to get firewood. Father Kino went back to camp and waited and watched. He went to the spring again. There were new tracks, but he saw no Indians.

Three, four, five days went by. The soldiers were busy and happy. There was good fishing and hunting of small game. It was a likely spot, this place Don Isidro had chosen. They cleared the ground and built a fort and a palm-thatched chapel. The fort they named in honor of Our Lady of Guadalupe. The chapel was Father Kino's first, and he inspected every palm frond that went into its building. He helped the men erect the altar, and no altar he had seen, he thought, was as beautiful as this one. On Palm Sunday he said Mass in his new chapel and gave Communion to the men and blessed palms for them.

Almost a week went by. The men began planting and the other tasks of pioneer living. Early one morning, with loud shouting and angry gestures, a band of Indians appeared at the newly-built fort. Wearing no clothing, their bodies covered only with war paint, and carrying bows and arrows, they came running into the encampment, looking very fierce and wild. Here truly were the heathens Father Kino had come to save. He was delighted; they were all that he had hoped for or expected.

He and Father Goñi went out to meet the Indians, offering them trinkets and ribbons and glass beads. They would not take the gifts from the hands of the priests, but made gestures showing that they wanted the gifts to be placed on the ground near them. This having been done, they picked up the things and examined them and were excited and pleased. Gradually they became more friendly.

Father Kino and Father Goñi walked among them and talked to them and gave them corn and bread. Then the priests got out their ink pots and quills and took down each sound, each syllable, each word an Indian uttered. Father Kino could not wait another hour to begin to learn their language. He showed them a crucifix and a statue of Our Lady of Guadalupe. They looked, but did not understand. Neither the cross nor the statue was familiar to them. Father Kino taught them to make the Sign of the Cross. This they did willingly enough. They had liked the presents and the bread and the corn that had been given them.

The Jesuit, making up his own sign language as he went along, invited the Indians to return the next day. Whether they understood his gestures or whether they were curious will never be known, but they did return, day after day, bringing new Indians with them and presents of firewood and fishnets.

Father Kino's days were not long enough to contain his great joy at the prospect of the harvest that was promised. The Indians seemed to him to be friendly and trusting and trustworthy, though the soldiers did not share his liking for nor his belief in the naked warriors. From the first they distrusted the Indians. They thought them crafty and to be feared. They were anxious that the redmen be made aware of Spanish authority and Spanish power.

Sermons and Masses and services of Holy Week were given in the leafy chapel. Father Kino wrote in his diary. He helped finish his little ranchito house, talked to the Indians in sign language, gave them corn and bread, and spent hours in prayer that they might receive the Christian teachings that he brought to them.

The Spaniards had finished building and planting. Now they hunted and fished and worked on the *Capitana*, caulking and repairing it. They walked short distances inland. Except for the spring they had found at their camp site, there seemed to be no other water supply.

Some of the supplies they had brought with them had spoiled, although there was still a comfortable amount left. The mainland could be seen from the shores of the Bay where they had built their fort. Atondo thought it a good idea to send the *Capitana* back for new supplies, for he believed in keeping a goodly amount on hand. Besides, he wanted horses for his men so that they could explore all of the inland country. And they had to find a greater water supply. This they could not do on foot. So the *Capitana* was repaired and sent back to the mainland near the end of April.

Father Kino noted in his diary that he had found some pretty shells which he thought were unusual. He began to write letters about a plan for pearl-fishing and about salt beds which he thought could be mined. Profits from both pearl-fishing and the salt beds could help with the expense of mission work. Even at this early date the far-seeing Kino feared that mission work might be discontinued because of its expense.

Learning the Indian language without an interpreter was slow work. Father Kino doubted the efficiency of teaching only through signs and requested and prayed that someone who knew both languages be sent to them.

A natural explorer, Father Kino went on trips with Don Isidro and the soldiers. He had interest and curiosity, and the fortitude for making new trails. Moreover, he knew what he was seeing. He made valuable maps which he sent back to Mexico and Spain.

Things moved slowly. Now that the building of the fort was completed, the men had more leisure time, which they spent in singing and playing the guitar and flute. This was good for them, for it kept them in a happy mood, but it was not good for the Indians. They sang and made music only in time of war—their flutes were part of their equipment for fighting—and music made them uneasy.

The Indians' uneasiness grew. They came daily to the fort, but they came with caution. Sometimes they brought their women and children with them. The women were timid and shy, but the children loved Father Kino. They called him Padre Eusebio and followed him everywhere.

Father Kino doubled his efforts at teaching the Indians, both adults and children. He performed his official duties as Royal Cosmographer and tended the spiritual needs of the men of the expedition. He was impatient and restless because he could not do more.

Time passed slowly. The *Capitana* was overdue. The Indians began stealing little things, which added to the Spaniards' distrust and dislike. Finally Don Isidro ordered a demonstration of the efficiency of Spanish firearms. The Indians were frightened and ran away. The next day, June 6th, they returned, a band of one hundred angry warriors, but Atondo frightened them away by shouting at them.

Supplies were low. The men were getting sick and afraid. Don Isidro suggested that he send the *Almeranta* to the mainland for new supplies and mail and word of the *Capitana*. The men would not hear of it. They would not consider being stranded on the island without a ship and demanded that the *Almeranta* be left with them.

The next day an Indian wounded a soldier. The wound was slight, but the act was serious. The Indians had defied Spanish authority. Don Isidro had the Indian captured and punished and imprisoned on shipboard.

All this time, there had been daily watches for the *Balandra*, the ship that had been left at Chacalo three months before. The *Capitana* did not return, and supplies were getting lower day by day.

The men were fearful and short-tempered. There were arguments and disputes. Someone punished the drummer boy and he ran away. Rumor spread like a grassfire through the encampment: the boy had been killed; the Indians had killed him.

The next day a group of Indians came to the fort making signs of peace, but the Spaniards did not believe them. They thought the Indians had come to rescue their tribesman who was imprisoned on shipboard. Fear and suspicion spread through the fort as quickly as had the rumor of the drummer boy's murder. It touched even the cool, level-headed Don Isidro.

He ordered that corn be given the visitors. As they ate it, sitting on the ground in the middle of the fort, Don Isidro ordered the cannon fired. Three Indians were killed. The others ran away in fright and disappeared in the woods near by. Father Kino could not believe that such a thing had come to pass. He had believed in Atondo, in his sense of justice, in his sound judgement. That these simple, child-like Indians had been killed as they were eating corn that had been given them was a thing that could not have happened—but it *had* happened. He had seen them die without ever having had a chance to know their God. Father Kino turned away, to walk in sorrow along the seashore where the angry waves slapped without ceasing against the sand.

Don Isidro called his men together. He wanted to send five men and the launch to the mainland for help. The men said no. Their refusal was firm and angry. They demanded that all of them be returned to the mainland at once. Don Isidro refused, for there were supplies left for seven days more. He said they would hold out as long as the supplies lasted. If by that time the *Balandra* or the *Capitana* had not made an appearance, he would allow the men to sail.

A week later, the supplies exhausted, all of the men, eighty-three in number, sailed from the Bay and in six days had reached the mainland.

The first Atondo expedition had ended in failure. What was especially heartbreaking was that the *Balandra*, having recovered from shipwreck, sailed into the Bay six days after this departure. They found the fort in ruins, the corn and beans still growing in the fields where the men had planted them. There were no signs of Indians; the place was deserted.

Atondo was disgusted and Kino, heartsick, but neither was discouraged. Atondo thought that fate had been against it; the men's fears had been against it. In his heart Father Kino believed that if they had stayed longer, if they could have made up to the Indians the terrible thing they had done to them, the story would have been a different one. But La Paz lay behind. The mistakes that had been made there were behind them. Eusebio Kino was not a man who looked backward.

Atondo knew that he had made mistakes, and he had learned important lessons from these mistakes. He meant to profit by them in a new adventure. He intended to try again. Some of the things he had learned were about outfitting an expedition. For this new one he wanted better equipment, more supplies, more men, more horses and mules and a fleet of canoes to go where sailing vessels could not sail. Don Isidro was a careful, efficient organizer. He sent the Viceroy long lists of what he wanted and the numbers and amounts necessary.

He wrote that he needed more soldiers and helmets and coats of mail for them. He wanted up-to-date arms and enough ammunition to supply each soldier for a year. He needed more sailors, and his three sailing vessels to be made seaworthy. He needed skilled craftsmen: blacksmiths, gunsmiths, caulkers. He needed Christianized Indians as scouts and he needed common laborers. He could use fifty young horses and horse armor for them. He needed saddles, pack-saddles, lariats, and hackamores. He needed good, strong mules as pack animals and responsible muleteers to take charge of them. He needed better anchors for his sailing vessels, axes, crowbars, shovels, knives, needles, thread, rope and hundreds of small things necessary for pioneer living. He needed provisions to last a year—and they must be better packed. Supplies had spoiled in his expedition because of poor packing. Atondo was not shy at telling what he needed. He wanted this expedition to succeed.

He knew it would take a long time for his request to be received by the Viceroy, reviewed by the proper persons, and possibly granted. It would take some time to get all the things together and at a port where he could pick them up.

Father Kino was impatient and kept urging Atondo to make a start of some kind while awaiting a reply from the Viceroy. Before the first expedition, Don Isidro had been a man of wealth, but he had spent his gold on that ill-fated venture. He still had jewels, silver and elaborate clothing. These he pledged toward expenses of the new venture. He followed this pledge by having an Englishman make him a fleet of canoes. This was a start, he told the impatient Kino.

Father Kino had nothing to pledge—no gold, silver, jewels, nor even extra clothing—but he knew where he could get help. So at once, in his usual hurry, he and Father Goñi set out to visit the many Jesuit missions established along the coast of the mainland. They, also, were not shy in asking for what they needed. Men of the Company of Jesus gave to men of the Company of Jesus. They were brothers, working for the same purpose. Each mission gave something: seeds, plants, trees, horses, mules, sheep, cattle. They gave what they could spare and added to it a like amount for extra measure.

Father Goñi got together a group of Christianized Mayo Indians who would join the expedition as laborers. What was more important, they would be good examples for the untamed tribes.

By the end of September a few of the things requested by Atondo were at the port of San Lucas waiting to be loaded. Some substitutions had been made, poor substitutions. Other things had not been sent at all. The arms were outmoded. There was not enough ammunition nor horseshoes nor nails for them. The anchors were not as good as Atondo had wanted. There were not enough helmets, coats of mail or horse armor.

But on the whole Atondo was pleased. He realized what a difficult undertaking it was to get these things together. The cities and ports of New Spain—Vera Cruz in Mexico, Mexico City, Guadalajara—had been called upon to furnish the things he had requested. Communication and transportation were slow and not trustworthy. The expedition was costing a frightening amount of money. Urged on by Father Kino, Atondo decided to sail with what he had. God willing, the remainder of the supplies and equipment would follow in a short time. He had the ships loaded and made ready to sail.

But where to go? The expedition, to be successful, must have land that could be planted in gardens and orchards, fields and pastures. There must be a climate suited to agriculture.

There must be a good and steady supply of water. There must be Indians who would allow them to stay.

About this time the long-overdue *Capitana* sailed into the port of San Lucas. The Captain told a tale of bad weather, high winds, terrific storms, and shipwreck with a loss of lives and cargo. He said that he had been forced to throw overboard more than a hundred horses, cattle and sheep. He ended his sad story with a bit of good news for Atondo and good promises for Father Kino. Near the place where he had thrown the stock into the waters of the Gulf was a river. There were many Indians living near by, and they were gentle and friendly.

This was what Don Isidro Atondo wanted to hear. Friendly Indians and a promise of a water supply was what he had been looking for these past months. Here it was! They would go to the mouth of this river. Father Kino was delighted.

The expedition set sail September 29th, 1683. On October 5th they reached their destination. On that day Father Kino and Father Goñi went ashore with Don Isidro Atondo to set up the cross and pray for God's blessing on their new undertaking.

The next day was the feast day of St. Bruno. According to Spanish custom, the new encampment in California was named San Bruno. He was its patron saint. On the feast day all the men went ashore. Father Kino said Mass with the sky the roof of his church and the sea roar his choir. Kneeling in the sand, the men received Communion. After Mass they prayed for strength to endure the hardships they knew lay ahead for them. They prayed for courage to face the dangers they knew they must face, and for health to survive. Father Kino prayed for souls to save.

When the prayers were finished, Father Kino and a small group of soldiers climbed a sharp hill to view the land. What they saw pleased them very much. The valley below was green and broad and flat. This was good for what had to be done. This second expedition must become self-supporting as quickly as possible. If this was to be accomplished, there must be flat and rich soil. The greenness of the valley seemed proof of rich soil. There was pasture for horses and mules, and trees for building and firewood. The river had water flowing between its banks.

They could see a good-sized Indian village only a few leagues away. This sight gave Father Kino joy. The Indian village would be his fertile valley.

Between the hill and the sea was the place chosen for the permanent fort. It seemed perfect for their needs.

In less than a month the fort was completed. The church was small, but it was Father Kino's delight. He made the altar himself, from some pretty stones that the Indians brought him. It was a precious thing; his loving hands had made it so. When it was finished, the Jesuit placed upon it a statue of Our Lady of Guadalupe, patroness of the Indians of Mexico. It was a day they treasured in memory.

Beside the church there was a house for the two priests. This house was the pride of the camp because it had a corridor and three good-sized sleeping rooms.

From the first days in camp, Indians had come to look at the strange white men and their horses and mules. They were friendly and gentle, as had been said of them. They were eager to learn all that Padre Eusebio had to teach them. They liked him, this man with a manner like their own friendly gentle ways. He was one of them. They felt it. They took him to their hearts. The children loved him and followed him wherever he went. They watched him as he prayed. They served him at Mass. They slept in his house at night. They were his little ones and he loved them in return.

The *Capitana* and the *Almeranta* sailed away to the mainland to get more pack mules and horseshoes and nails, to get more men and supplies. Those who were left in camp settled into a routine that patterned their days. In the morning there was Angelus and Mass, and then each man went to the task that had been given him. At evening time there was Angelus and Rosary. Then, far into the night, the two Jesuit Fathers taught the red-skinned people, communicating as best they could.

To the north and west and south there were settlements of Indians, three great tribes. Sometimes there was peace among them, but most of the time there was war or rumor of war. Each tribe feared and distrusted the other two, but they were friendly with the men of the expedition. They loved the black-robed priest. Ibo, chief of the southern tribe, was a tall, strong, powerful man. He and Father Kino became friends. Because of this friendship, Ibo moved part of his tribe to San Bruno. These men were willing workers; the Spanish approved of them.

Now that the fort was completed and promising with its plantings and teachings, Atondo decided to explore. One of the accomplishments of this expedition was to be the exploration inland across Lower California to its western coast.

Father Kino was anxious to go with the exploring party. Although, like everyone else, he called California the largest island in the world, he was not sure that it was an island. Perhaps something along the route of exploration might prove him right or wrong.

They called these exploring trips Entradas, and there were to be four of them. Their purpose was to find water holes and to make friends with the Indians. Father Kino went along as chaplain and mapmaker, but his greatest contribution was his gift for making friends. No matter how frightened the Indians became at their first sight of men in mail and leather armor, riding armored horses, Father Kino could ease their fear. His coat of mail was his courage, his goodness and his love for Indian people. Indians everywhere sensed this and loved and trusted him in return. No red hand was ever turned against him.

While some of the men were out on these exploring trips, others had sailed to the mainland for supplies. The rest remained at San Bruno to finish building and to plant crops, orchards and gardens. At first the planting had given promise, for there was some river water for irrigation and some rainfall, but as time went on the days became hot and dry. There was no rain, no moisture in the air. The river became a dry bed. Hot winds buried the new struggling plants in hills of sand. The men kept on working and praying. The missionaries prayed with them. This expedition must not fail.

Chapter 7

THE DAYS DRAGGED ON. The sun beat down upon the land. Hot winds blew the sands across the valleys. Heat waves misted the distance. There were no clouds, no rain, no shade. Rivers disappeared in the dry sand; water holes became dry.

The exploring parties kept on, breaking trails across the land. The Indians along the way were starving, for their crops had withered and died. They were eating plant roots and seeds. They watched the horses and the mules and could not hide their hunger. There was always danger that they would steal and eat the animals.

The exploring parties kept on, becoming larger as more foot soldiers and Indians trotted behind the horsemen. They traveled for longer times and for greater distances. Atondo led each of the four Entradas. Father Kino went on most of them. Another post, San Isidro, was built at the site of a spring a few leagues from San Bruno.

Each time when the men returned to San Bruno, footsore, discouraged, aching with fatigue, they found little at the post to comfort them. The two sailing ships had returned, bringing some supplies, mules and horses, but not enough. They were sent back again and again.

On one of the trips to the mainland, Father Kino went along to get help from his brother Jesuits in the Mexico missions. As always, he was successful. They gave him what they could. It helped, but there was never enough of anything. Transporation was slow and not to be relied upon.

The exploring parties from San Bruno kept on. Men who were too tired or too ill to continue traveling were left at the post. Other soldiers took their places on the Entradas. Atondo would not give up. This fourth expedition had to succeed. He was determined to reach the Pacific.

Only Father Kino was happy. He seemed never to grow weary, never to be hungry, never to be discouraged. He could ride all day and teach and pray all night. Each group of Indians they met along the way added to his eagerness to convert them. The Indians responded to his gentle zeal, begging for baptism, for the Sacraments. They begged him to stay and teach them. Each dry water hole that he saw today became in his imagination a thriving mission of tomorrow, with water in plenty and souls in need.

He baptized the babies and the dying. The others must wait to become fully instructed, to know right from wrong, to be able to live by the faith he gave them. He must give them this faith. He must return to each group that he met along the way. This was his constant prayer—to return . . . to return. The Indians ran after him as he rode away, begging him to stay . . . to stay.

The fourth Entrada was the largest of all: four men in coats of mail, twenty-nine soldiers, two blacksmiths, two muleteers, two parties of scouts and an uncounted number of Indian guides and laborers. There were nine Christian

Indians, five horses in metal armor, and twenty-two in armor made of bullhide. Thirty pack mules carried provisions, supplies, Father Kino's astronomical instruments, his church vessels and vestments and gifts for the Indians.

On march, the pattern of the days was much the same. The scouts went first to view the land and decide the route of travel. They returned to the night camp to report. Father Kino went with them with his telescope and his cheerful heart. At dawn each morning, soldiers and Indians followed the scouts to open the trail for the horses and mules. They cut down trees and underbrush and dug up roots. With crowbars they pried huge boulders from the line of march. They leveled the too-steep inclines. They filled in the holes where boulders and tree roots had been. At dusk they returned to camp—weary, footsore, dust-covered, sunburned and blistered. While they had been gone, the blacksmiths had been busy. They had pared the horses' hoofs and shod them, trying to make do with the heartbreaking shortage of horseshoes and nails.

Each morning, the night camp moved forward. For most of the day it was necessary that the soldiers walk and lead their horses. Besides pulling reluctant horses along the stony trail, the soldiers had other worries. Each man had to carry his own equipment, consisting of a heavy leather jacket, bullhide armor and shield, arquebus, powder, balls, slugs and a gourd of water.

Sometimes the trail led along a narrow rock ledge. When a soldier looked up, he could see a thousand feet of sheer rock cliff. When he looked down, he saw a boulder-filled canyon a thousand feet below. Many of the horses fell from the narrow ledge and were dashed to pieces on the rocks below. Others became so lame that they had to be left on the trail for the Indians to find.

The pack mules were afraid and stubborn. They refused to go forward or backward. They balked on the trail. Soldiers had to push and pull them. There was always danger that the frightened animals would stampede. Some of the packs were lost, shaken off by the frightened and saddle-sore mules.

Often the trail came to a dead end against a rock-walled mountain. If there was a possible way around, the men went around. If the way led up a dry river bed, they plodded along through the deep sand.

Every step of the way was difficult and dangerous, but never dull. A new world opened daily before the marching men. Each hour brought discovery. Each league brought excitement. Once they passed through a section which the Indians called the Land of the Giants. Even the Spaniards saw—or thought they saw—giant tracks.

Everywhere the men went, different Indian tribes told them about the Lady in Blue. They said she walked across the wasteland and the wild country, always alone. She was not an Indian, they said, but fair and beautiful. When they shot arrows into her body, she did not fall. She kept on walking.

Father Kino was interested. He wondered about these strange tales he heard and the strange things he saw. He kept a diary and made detailed maps.

At last the fourth Entrada reached the Pacific Ocean. The sea was smooth and beautiful. The men were overjoyed at having reached it. Father Kino went walking on the shore to see what he could see. He found a piece of iron; someone from Europe had been here before him. He found whale bones and sea shells. The shells especially interested him. Some of them were rose-colored. Others were blue, of brilliant luster, and so large that the Indians used them for bowls.

Don Isidro Atondo had accomplished one thing that he had set out to do: he had opened a trail from the Gulf across Lower California to the shores of the Pacific Ocean. The expedition rested here for a short time and then returned to where they had left the soldiers and Indians and horses and mules.

The way back to San Bruno was easier and quicker than the forward march had been. On the return trip the Indians along the trail welcomed them back. Several times they showed the men a new and shorter route of travel. All of the Indians begged Father Kino to stay with them. He could not at this time, he told them, but he would return. He dreamed of a chain of missions across the land with many Jesuit Fathers caring for the Indians. He would return; other Jesuits would follow him. He promised this to himself. He promised it to the Indians. He prayed that God would will it to pass.

When the men arrived back at San Bruno, they met a sorrowful sight. Most of those who had been left at the post, as well as the Indians, were dangerously ill, paralyzed and dying. An epidemic of scurvy was taking its toll. Supplies were nearly exhausted. Almost at once the men who had returned also became ill.

No expedition was worth the lives of the loyal men, both white and Indian, who had come with him, said Atondo. There was nothing to do but bury the dead and load the paralyzed and dying on shipboard. He sent them back to the mainland, to the Jesuit missions along the Mexican coast. There the good Fathers would nurse them to health again, if that was possible, or if not, they would give them Christian burial in a Christian country.

Also waiting for Atondo was a letter from the Viceroy complaining about the cost of the expedition. It had cost the Spanish King a quarter of a million dollars. What did Atondo have to show for it? A few trails opened? A few Indian babies baptized? Was that enough for such a cost? Atondo read the letter to the end. He showed it to Father Kino. The priest read it and prayed that God in His mercy would not forsake his Indian children who begged to be taught His Word.

The year was 1685.

Chapter 8

ON MAY SEVENTH San Bruno and San Isidro were abandoned. The Spaniards had finished with California. They had given it all they had: their dreams, their strength, their health. Many had given their lives. Those who still lived were too ill to grieve because an expedition had failed. They were too ill to care that Indians had been shown a better way of life and then that way had been taken from them. They were through.

But Father Kino was not through. He had promised his Indian children that he would return, and his heart was in agony at the thought that he would not be allowed to keep that promise. Everywhere he turned he could see in memory the Indians running after him as he rode away. He could hear in memory their cries begging him to stay. Surely it would be God's will that he be returned to them.

He prayed and Atondo hoped. Atondo had given his wealth and his word that he would explore, colonize and Christianize California. He was not ready to admit defeat.

Father Kino had no feeling of defeat. The Indians of California were his friends, his spiritual children. They wanted and needed what he could give them. If one way failed, there were other ways to try. He would try all of them.

There were always men ready and eager to go on an expedition. There were other places in California which might be better suited for agriculture. Father Kino could get supplies from the Jesuit missions on the mainland, and there was also the possibility of pearl-fishing. For more than a hundred years there had been pearl-fishing and pearl fishermen on the Gulf coast. Perhaps they could pay for a new expedition with the pearls they might find. Father Kino, always optimistic, was certain they would. Don Isidro, in desperation, was willing to try.

On May 8th Don Isidro and Father Goñi sailed for Sinaloa to get divers and outfit themselves for a pearl-fishing expedition. A few hours later, Father Kino and Captain Guzman sailed to get supplies from the Jesuit missions.

It did not take Atondo long to get his divers and get back to the California coast. All through the hot August and September days they dived for oysters. Crewmen and Indians helped. They brought up enormous quantities of oysters, but few pearls and most of these were of poor quality. Up and down the lower Gulf coast Atondo sailed, trying every inlet and bay and island. Many oysters but few pearls were the result.

Meanwhile Father Kino had gathered his supplies from the different Jesuit missions. In June he and Guzman sailed up the coast of Mexico to spend three days with the Seri Indians. As usual, Father Kino was to win them completely. They begged him to stay with them. They would give him horses and provisions, they said, and would help him build a fort and a church.

Father Kino promised to return, if he were given permission. He dreamed of establishing a mission for the Seri which would help supply the desolate land of Lower California when he returned there, for he was determined to return.

When Father Kino and Guzman reached San Bruno, they found that the eighteen-months' drought had been broken. The spring was full and the waters of the river were flowing again. Best of all, the Indians still wanted their Padre Eusebio to stay with them.

Back in Mexico, Father Kino wrote to the Bishop begging for permission to return to his work in California. Neither the drought nor the scurvy epidemic had been limited to California, he wrote. Mexico and all of New Spain had suffered. This might not happen again for many years. If they went back to California, argued Father Kino, everything might be in their favor. Besides, the Indians needed what the Spanish could give them, and how terrible it was to want the Word of God and be deprived of it.

Father Kino also wrote to the Bishop and to the Viceroy suggesting ways of cutting down expenses of a new expedition. He and Atondo had worked out a plan calling for fewer men and horses, less equipment, fewer supplies. The cost of such an expedition could be kept within thirty thousand dollars a year.

After many conferences, the plan was accepted. The Viceroy sent a message saying that they were willing to have it tried out. The California missions would be kept open for another smaller expedition, and Don Isidro Atondo and Father Eusebio Kino were to be in complete authority.

Father Kino lost no time in celebration. A prayer of thanksgiving, and he was ready to plan and organize. He urged Don Isidro to hurry, hurry. Time must not be wasted.

Suddenly, without warning, a royal order came from Spain. All preparation for an expedition to California was to be stopped. California mission work must be stopped at once. A royal order was the final word.

But not for Father Eusebio Francisco Kino. This way closed, quickly he asked God's help in opening another way. The California Indians must not be abandoned. Now he saw a way that would enable him to help both California and the Seri Indians. If he could be sent to the Seri country, his dream of having these Indians help their California brothers could become a reality. So he asked to be sent either among the Seri or the Guaymas, who also wanted him. Permission was granted. The realization of his dream lay at his finger tips.

There was something Father Kino had to do before he went to them. For a long time it had grieved him that many Indians were forced into labor. He wanted this stopped. How could the Indians accept Christianity wholeheartedly when men professing this same faith abused and enslaved them? It must be stopped. Now he set off for Guadalajara to see what he could do about it.

He went at once to the *Audiencia* and asked for a paper with the royal Seal of Authority to prohibit Christianized Indians from enforced labor, especially in the silver mines. He was prepared for long and reasonable argument, argument which he was determined to win. Surprisingly, he received the paper at once and without question. He immediately left for his new field of labor, armed with the paper giving freedom to his new children.

The way to the Gulf led through the mountains and the foothills. It was a rough, rocky road to travel, long and lonely for one man on muleback. Many nights Father Kino slept in the open, with no comforts other than his saddle blanket and his saddle. Sometimes he stayed at ranchos or in towns or missions along the way. He tried to plan his day's trip so as to arrive at one of these by nightfall. Sometimes he was successful; more often he was not. He almost always carried his water supply from one camp site to the next. Occasionally there were water holes near the trail, but he was afraid to risk not finding one. His daily ration of jerky and tortillas he could do without, if need be. He was indifferent to food, but water was a necessity.

It took Father Kino almost two months to reach a mining town which was opposite the California coast where he had begun the missions. The town was rich and booming; its silver mines were the greatest in the region. They had been discovered about the time the California missions had been abandoned. Father Kino was certain that the discovery of the rich veins of silver here was God's way of showing that the California missions could be kept open. The land was giving what was needed to take care of its people. He thought this was a sign that God's blessing would be on his work with the Seri and the Guaymas, and he hurried on his way to get the good work started.

He rode on to Father Gonzales' mission. Because distances were so great, Father Gonzales had been given authority to make decisions for this part of the Jesuit world, and Father Kino went to him to get instructions before leaving for the Seri country. Also visiting there was Father Aguilar, whose mission, Cucurpe, was the last one on the border of the Pimería Alta, that unknown, unexplored country of uncounted leagues.

For fifty years the Jesuits had been working in Mexico, which they had explored as far as Cucurpe mission in Sonora. The country had been partly settled, and some of the Indians had been Christianized. The Jesuit missions were adjoined by haciendas, which they used as supply centers for the mission Indians and also to help in the establishment of new missions. Cucurpe was such a place, with its church, its hacienda, and its near-by Indian village.

Beyond this was the Pimería Alta: vast, arid, mountainous land in northern Mexico and what is now southern Arizona, extending from the Altar River to the Gila, from the San Pedro River to the Gulf of California and to the Colorado River on the west. It was inhabited by thousands of Indians who had seldom or never seen a white man.

They belonged to four powerful tribes, the largest and most important group of which were the Pimas, whose villages lay in the valleys of the Gila and Salt Rivers. Both the Pimas and the Sobaípuris—who were related to them but lived under a different tribal organization—lived by hunting small game and by agriculture. Their houses were brush shelters, their utensils woven baskets, their beds woven mats. They wove cotton for their clothing.

To the west were the Papago tribe, related to the Pimas and Sobaípuris. All three tribes spoke a different dialect, though their language had the same root. The Papago were much like their relatives, but not so progressive. While they knew about irrigation, for example, they did not practice it as did the other two tribes, but planted their small crops in dry washes and river beds where water flowed in the growing rainy season. They, too, wove baskets and cotton for clothing and hunted small game. In addition, they traded salt which they took from their salt lagoons.

The fourth great group was made up of the Yuman tribes who spoke a different language from the Piman group. They raised some crops, but did not have irrigation. Their houses were primitive grass shelters. They wore little clothing, were very poor, and not as progressive as their neighbors.

Although all of these groups raided one another occasionally and had small battles from time to time, they were not warlike, but gentle and trusting people unless roused to anger. Like the Spanish, they feared the nomad Apaches, who wandered on the outskirts of the Pimería Alta, savagely raiding, stealing, and killing.

Now a report had reached Mexico City that the people of the Pimería Alta were growing restless. There was a hint of uprising. Spain and Mexico were worried, for the Pueblo rebellion in New Mexico was scarcely over—town criers were still giving news of the cruelty and torture of that bloody time—and an Indian rebellion could happen again. Moreover, in the Pimería Alta there were many more thousands of Indians than in the Pueblo country, and an uprising would no doubt be more violent.

The government was looking for ways to quiet the Pimería Alta people. They needed a leader who was responsible and trustworthy. At the same time the Jesuits were eager to extend their line of missions past Cucurpe, into the Pimería Alta and to the Apache frontier. They needed a pioneer missionary priest to begin the work of Christianizing the Piman and Yuman people, a man of vision whom they could trust and whom the Indians could love.

Dispatches, letters, messages from Spain to Mexico City, from Guadalajara to Sonora went back and forth. Church and government officials held talks; names were mentioned; work was compared and accomplishments examined. In every letter and dispatch, at every meeting and conference, one name led the rest—but the final decision had been left to Father Gonzales. Father Aguilar had not come from Cucurpe for a social visit but to ask Father Gonzales to send back with him a missionary to go into the unknown land beyond his mission.

Into this situation rode Father Kino, asking for final orders to take with him to the Seri. Father Gonzales liked him immediately, and the friendship which grew between the two priests lasted for many years. As Father Aguilar looked at and listened to the man sitting opposite him at the table, he prayed that this would be his missionary neighbor. Father Gonzales was busy with his own thoughts. He listened, answered questions, and joined in the conversation, but a part of his mind was elsewhere. Was this Father Kino all that he seemed to be, all that others believed of him? Was he fearless, determined, to be counted on for good judgement and justice in his dealing with the Indians? Finally Father Gonzales decided that Eusebio Kino was all of these things. He made his decision, and at last he spoke. Father Kino was not to go to the Seri or to the Guaymas; the California Indians would have to wait for another shepherd. Father Kino must go to the Pimería Alta.

At first Father Kino could not believe he had heard correctly. He was not to go to the Seri? He was never to keep his promise and return to the California Indians? But this was the decision. Father Gonzales had spoken, and Eusebio Kino knew how to obey. He spent the remainder of the night in church asking St. Francis Xavier to obtain divine help for him. If this was to be his work, he would give it all he had—his body, his mind and his heart.

By dawn the next morning the three priests were in the saddle riding to Cucurpe, fifty leagues away. They remained there overnight, and, although Father Aguilar was anxious that the new missionary stay for a day or two, Father Kino would not hear of it. He was impatient to see the Pima country, to meet the people with whom he hoped to spend the rest of his days.

So again at dawn the three were jogging along the trail. Though it was early in March, the day was hot and breathless. The desert stretching ahead of them was silent and still. No winds stirred the clumps of wild grass or the mesquite trees. Before too long the riders entered the land of the giant cactus. These tall gaunt saguaros were lonely sentinels in an almost empty land. The priests rode single file, each one lost in the prayers of his own heart. Their black robes were gray with desert sand. Clouds of sand engulfed them, stinging their eyes, parching their throats. But Father Kino was at peace. His prayers of the night had washed away his disappointment of yesterday's decision. God in His good time would help him bring the Holy Faith to the Indians of California. He was certain of this. He rode with serenity into the sun-filled day.

Chapter 9

AT MIDDAY the priests reached Cosari, beyond the settled frontier. The people were waiting for them. Father Aguilar had sent a runner to tell them that their priest was coming, and now they came along the trail to welcome the three missionaries, especially the one who would be theirs. They explained that Coxi, their chief, was away. If he had been at home, he would have led them in their welcome. Father Kino was touched at their courtesy and their welcome.

Until late in the afternoon he talked with the people. He showed them a beautiful painting which he had brought for them. Juan Correa, one of Mexico's most famous artists, had given it to him almost a year before, to be placed on the altar of his first church in his new field. The picture was of Our Lady of Sorrows, *Nuestra Señora de los Dolores*. This would be the name of the church he would build here, he told the Indians. It would be dedicated to her, and she would be their friend and their patroness.

In late afternoon the priests rode out from the village for a quiet hour before the time for evening instruction at the village. The sun had eased its way across the cloudless sky. Purple shadows rested in the distant foothills, and the faraway mountains pushed against the edge of the valley. The little river, the San Miguel, that they had followed from the mission at Cucurpe, trickled its way through its sandy bed. Suddenly it dropped into a deep rock canyon. Father Kino rode along the edge, looking deep down to the canyon floor where the river now splashed and churned in its rocky bed. Almost as suddenly as it had dropped into the canyon, it flowed out again into a wide, green meadow. To the east and the west and closing its lower end, the mountains cupped the meadow land.

Father Kino reined his mule and looked with delight at the *vegas* before him. The land lay peaceful and lovely and rich in promise. Far to his right was the Indian village. At his feet, above the flowing San Miguel and the green meadow, was a small high mesa. On this small rock he would build his church of Dolores.

As if it lay completed before him, Father Kino saw his finished mission. He saw the buildings and the orchards and the fields, the corrals and the pasture lands. He saw his church, Nuestra Señora de los Dolores. It would be the Mother of Missions for all the other ones he would build across the vast Pimería Alta.

He dismounted and knelt in the shadows of early evening. His thoughts flashed backward. He was again the boy from Segno pausing on the trail to look while the bell rang out for Angelus. Only this time he was looking forward, not backward. This time the Angelus was evening, not morning. But his prayer was the same. He said it now. "The Angel of the Lord declared unto Mary. . . . now and at the hour of our death. . . ."

His two companions, kneeling, answered him.

The next morning Father Gonzales left to ride back to his own mission, elated. He felt that God had guided him in the decision he had made, that He was pleased because Eusebio Kino would carry His Word to the Pimas.

After they had received Father Gonzales' blessing and had watched him start the long trail back, Father Kino and Father Aguilar also rode off, westward over the mountains. They visited and were welcomed at three large Indian villages on the way back to Dolores. The people had heard of the blackrobes who had come into the country south of them and were pleased that these things would now be theirs. They welcomed the man who would bring them.

Father Kino listened and accepted their welcome and looked and dreamed and planned. This country would be his starting place. He would begin here. He would build four great missions at each of the villages they had visited: Caborca (now San Ignacio), Imuris, Cocóspera, Remedios. He planned them. He saw them in completion. This area consisted of only a hundred leagues or so, a small dot in the vastness of the Pimería Alta. Still it was a beginning. Once these missions were completed and the Indians who lived near them converted and trained, he would go farther into the unknown.

The two priests rode each day, all day. They went from village to village. Through the long hours of the night, they instructed the people, comforted the sick, anointed the dying. Babies were brought to them to be baptized.

Slowly they made the circuit from Dolores to Caborca to Imuris to Cocóspera to Remedios to Dolores. As they jogged along the trail, Father Kino mapped every league of the way. He was detailed, careful and accurate. He was interested in everything he saw, and he saw everything. He was interested in the land, its geography, its resources, its climate. He was interested in the people, where they lived and how they lived. He was interested in their customs and their beliefs.

He remembered the day on a hill near an Indian village, where he had found a great hole in the ground with massive boulders wedged in its opening. He learned that the

Indians believed that this was the Cave of the Winds. Only the boulders held the wild winds within it captive. If they were removed, the Indians believed, and the wild winds freed, terrible storms would rage across their land.

The priest had not laughed at this belief. It was important because the Indians believed it. The Indians were important because they were people and what they believed was a part of them. He reported what he heard, making little or no comments. Like his maps, his diaries were detailed, careful and accurate. They became valuable pieces of history for the people who came after him.

Finally the missionaries arrived back at Cosari where the mother mission of Dolores was to be built. Father Aguilar had to leave from here. His own people and his own mission needed him. Although they had been almost two weeks in the saddle every day and busy with religious duties every night, Father Aguilar seemed refreshed. He felt spiritually renewed. It had been an experience he would never forget, this being so closely in touch with the serious, dedicated, restless Father Kino. It was an experience he would repeat, he promised himself, whenever opportunity offered.

Father Kino rode along the trail behind Father Aguilar for a league or so. It was his way of saying, "*Vaya con Dios.*" But at last he reined his mule, for it was time to turn back. He had work to do.

Father Aguilar sat in his saddle, watching his brother in God ride back along the trail they had come. Finally he turned, going in the opposite direction, but his thoughts were with his new friend who went so joyously to his new work in the little-known, untamed land of the Upper Pima.

When Father Kino came within sight of his green meadow where Dolores Mission would be, he dismounted and stood looking at the distant mountain cupping his valley. Suddenly he laughed. This man who was not given to laughter, who was always too much in a hurry, laughed again. Startled, his mule looked back at him. Kino gave it a slap, to start it on its way. If his feet talked to the land as they should, he told himself, he, being a man of the Tyrol, would arrive back at his village before the sun had fully risen.

In Cosari, as it had been with the Indians of California, Father Kino was loved by the children. They called him Padre Eusebio and followed him wherever he went. When he rode muleback, as many as could rode behind his saddle; the rest followed as closely as they dared. Even the little girls were never too far away. They hid in the mesquite trees, their dark faces peering out through its lacy leaves. They squatted behind the cholla cactus, their black eyes watching him. They stood beside the flame bush and the palo-verde, forever giggling in admiration, their small hands hiding their mouths, their gaze following their beloved Padre.

At first it had been only the children who went where their new priest went. The older Indians had welcomed him when he first came and now they watched him. They listened when he spoke, although they understood only the tone of his voice. They tried to understand his sign language. They tried to anticipate his desires and needs. But they were shy people. They did not give themselves to loving him as quickly as their children did. At first, they were content with watching. But from his first day they tried to do what he told them to do. They were glad to help him. Not completely understanding what he wanted, they tried to give it to him.

When he went into the mountains looking

for trees that could give him lumber for the new church, the Indians showed him their tallest and straightest. When he walked along the river bank, rubbing bits of soil between his fingers, they seemed to know what he wanted to find. At once they took him to a clay pit where clay for adobe bricks could be had for the making.

When Padre Eusebio said Mass, the people watched him. Their black eyes moved with his movements. When he walked before his shelter, they watched him. They watched him read his Breviary. They watched his lips as he prayed.

They were fascinated with the things his hands did so well and beautifully. They watched the strength and quickness of his hands as they chopped the trees and sawed the trunks into board lengths and planed the boards. They watched his hands, their gentleness, as he blessed the babies and the dying. They watched the dedication of his hands as he raised the Host in Holy Sacrifice.

Suddenly they knew reverence. They were made to know that here before them was no ordinary man. He was not as they were. He was consecrated to Something greater than they had ever known. Gradually they came to understand that what he had, he offered to them. Then hearts opened to him and they loved him. They loved him with a childlike love. They joined their children to follow him wherever he went.

It had been the middle of March the morning Padre Eusebio walked back to Cosari, leading his mule. By the middle of April he had built, the Indians helping him, a small simple church. Beside the church he had built his house, a single room. There he slept briefly each night, his saddle blanket his bed, his saddle his pillow.

In between his days of labor and his nights of instructing his people, he was always riding away somewhere. He never rode alone. Always the small boys went with him, running before him, beside him, behind him through the deep sands of the trail. Always the little girls followed him as far as they dared to go. Then they waited in silent patience until he came back again.

Near the end of April Father Kino again made the circuit of his missions-to-be. The Indians he met welcomed him as they had the first time, but they were a shy and reserved people. Father Kino knew that he would have to live with them before he could win them completely to trust in him and in the ways of God.

For the next six years he managed to go almost every week to these villages, baptizing, instructing. He also made many trips back to Cucurpe and to Ures, where Father Roxes was in charge. These visits were begging trips to ask his brothers for things that he needed to get his new mission of Dolores started.

Father Roxes gave him provisions, horses and a little silver. But his most valuable gift was the two men he sent to work with Father Kino. One of these was an interpreter who could be trusted to make honest and true translations of what Father Kino said and what was said to him. With this Indian went his blind brother who became a wonderful teacher and whom Father Kino learned to value as his best helper.

During these first mission-begging expeditions Father Kino brought back seeds, plants, young trees. Back at Dolores he planned gardens, orchards, fields. He had the Pimas plant all the crops they knew about and many that they did not know. Before long they harvested a goodly garden crop. Their trees bore fruits; apricots, peaches, figs, quinces and pomegranates.

When he went to Cucurpe, Father Kino

asked for baby animals and proudly carried back to Dolores young calves and colts, lambs and sucklings.

As time went on, the children's Padre rode longer distances to farther-away missions, and he never returned empty-handed. He and the boys who followed him went to all the sleepy little Mexican towns throughout Sonora. They went to all the elegant ranches and rich haciendas.

As soon as he could, Father Kino established a supply of goods that he could use as money for labor and trade. He found that cotton cloth, hand-woven blankets, corn and wheat were valued more than silver money. So he began teaching his people to grow and to make these things. Soon the mission of Dolores was a beehive of activity. Men dug foundations for new buildings. They dug out rock from the canyon ledges and the river bed, hauled them back over the trail to fill in the foundation trenches they had dug.

They went into the mountains to chop down the tall pine trees and haul them back to the building site. Men, horses and mules did the hauling. The Indians owned no wagons. When the logs were brought to the mission, they were sawed into board lengths and stacked in piles to season. Men and women trampled straw into the wet clay to make adobe. These were molded by hand into bricks and stacked where the hot desert sun could burn them dry and hard. Other groups learned to make the tiles that were used in the roofs. These were baked in the kiln they had made. Not all the roofs were tile roofs; many were dirt-filled, trampled to hardness.

It seemed as if everything Padre Eusebio touched or tended, planted or built, yielded its harvest. All the years of his boyhood and early schooling, his later training and years of rigid discipline, his waiting and disappointments had been but a preparation and a slow growing period for all this that was happening now.

Every day he taught the Pimas to build strong foundations, straight walls, tight roofs. At night he instructed them, baptized them, gave them the Sacraments. He gave them a Holy Faith and taught them devotion to it.

Slowly, day by day, month by month, the mission of Dolores grew. When the time came that he needed more workers than he could find in the village of Cosari, Father Kino sent runners to other Pima villages, inviting the people to come to learn how to work and how to live a Christian way of life. They came by the hundred.

Padre Eusebio sent to Mexico for chalices and other church vessels, for ornaments and vestments. He sent for crucifixes and holy water fonts, for holy pictures and statues of the saints. He sent for church bells. Although by now the Indians were building a larger church, the bells were placed on the small tower of the first simple chapel. In all their years the Pimas had heard few bells before. They loved them. Not only at Angelus, but on every occasion that gave the least excuse, they rang them. The bells pealing across the flat, hot land swelled in the stillness of the hot, unmoving air. The people listened to them with pleasure and delight.

The Indians who were being trained as carpenters made doors and window frames for all of the buildings. The women plastered all the outside walls with plaster made of cream-thick clay. They trampled the inside clay floors to the hardness of stone. With rubbing stones they polished the hard clay floors until they shone with the luster of mahogany.

Pack trains came and went along the deep-cut trail by the river. Mules kicked up clouds of flying sand that chased the whirlwinds into the shadows of the foothills.

The church and the convento were almost finished. The patios and inner patios had been planted with vegetables and flowers. Vines curtained the open corridors. Trees shaded the pathways of the cloister. To the back were the washrooms, the carpenter shop, the weaving room, the kilns, the kitchen and the kitchen storerooms. Farther back were the forges, the watermill and the storehouses for wheat and corn. Along the side were the offices of government, the school, the trading post and the house shelters of the workmen.

Before Father Kino had come to them, the Pimas had known something about building, about planting and irrigation and about weaving cotton and fibers. He taught them to perfect these skills. He also taught them new skills. He trained carpenters and blacksmiths and gunsmiths. He taught them how to breed and raise domesticated animals. Under his skillful management there developed at Dolores great horse herds, cattle herds, great flocks of sheep. He trained horsemen and cowboys and shepherds. He taught them how to round-up and brand and butcher.

Father Kino organized a system of government and taught his people how to govern themselves. He gave them The Cane of Authority and taught them responsibility, justice and fairness.

It took six years to complete the mission of Nuestra Señora de los Dolores, but long before Dolores was completed Father Kino had begun building the missions of Remedios and Cocóspera. The pack trains from Dolores cut deep trails going back and forth to the two new missions. Besides horses, cattle, wheat and corn, the Indians took flour, meal, lard and tallow.

Even before its completion, Dolores had become Mother of Missions for Padre Eusebio's Pimería Alta.

The year was 1692.

Chapter 10

WORK DID NOT TAKE up all the time. There were the holy-days to be celebrated, and important events that must be marked in fitting manner. Both the Indians and their neighbors, Mexican and Spanish, loved pomp and ceremony. Although Father Kino was austere in his personal habits, he, too, loved ceremony in paying homage to God and to His angels and saints. For fiesta occasions nothing was too elaborate, nothing too festive.

Perhaps without realizing it, the good Father missed the Old World elegance of Trent, of Ingolstadt and Munich, of Innsbruck and Hall, of Milan and Seville. For many years his days had been spent in cities rich in medieval splendor where Kings and Queens, men of letters, of music, of the arts lavished their wealth and jewels, their books of learning, their songs, their paintings and their sculpture in the glory of God.

Here in the Pimería Alta the desert was barren of splendor. Its only majesty was its emptiness, its silence and its distances. There were no Kings and Queens in all New Spain. There were scholars, musicians, artists and sculptors in Mexico City, but Mexico City was months away by trail and horseback.

What there was, Father Kino assembled for his pageantry. The wives of the rich mine owners and haciendados had some jewels and velvets. There were good primitive painters and primitive carvers. There were homemade stringed instruments, drums of skin, bone whistles and flutes whose music was as sweet as angels' harps. The Indian choir Father Kino had trained sang the High Mass as perfectly as any choir in Europe. The Indians with the vivid, strong, barbaric colors of their headdresses and banners and shields gave drama to any gathering.

And there were the simple things that Father

Kino loved so deeply: the crosses and wreaths and arches made of pine boughs and palo-verde and flame bush, gifts of the desert straight from the heart of the desert people.

Father Kino's first celebration took place shortly after his arrival at Cosari. Easter was in March that year, and the little church he and the Indians were building could not possibly be finished in time to celebrate the Resurrection of Christ with High Mass. Father Aguilar of Cucurpe and Father Roxes of Ures came to his rescue. They would celebrate Easter Mass at a church midway between their missions and the new one being built at Dolores. All the Indians from the three areas were invited to come. The Mexican and Spanish families from miles away were invited.

Father Kino and a hundred of his new converts walked in procession all the way. At their head were forty small children—"the littlest Christians," their Padre called them—and the Spanish ladies loved them and made much of them, dressing them for the occasion in their own velvets and laces.

There was a greater celebration when the famed and loved Chief Coxi of Dolores and his two sons embraced the Holy Faith and were baptized at Dolores.

But the largest and most gala was the celebration that took place when the mission at Dolores was completed. It had taken six years to build, and its dedication was a day of festival to be remembered by the Pimas and their children and their grandchildren. The church was finished. The bells had been placed in the bell tower. The altar had its proper linens, its proper vessels. Church dignitaries from Mexico City and Sonora led the procession before High Mass in vestments heavy with jewels and gold embroidery. Heads of State came in crimson velvet carrying banners with royal coats-of-arms. The military were present, stiff in regimental uniforms, presenting arms, marching in formation. Haciendados came, correct in dress, haughty in manner. Mine owners were accompanied by their wives and children, beautiful in laces and silks from Spain.

The Indians made the greatest showing, with their headdresses of many colored feathers, their bright-hued blankets, their painted bodies. The Pimas walked in pride because this was their mission, their blackrobe, their Padre. The Sobaípuris and the Papago stood in silent groups, a little apart, curious and envious. The Yuman tribes had sent their representatives. They came in peace this time. Even a few Apache lurked in the background, watching everything.

Padre Eusebio sang High Mass. His altar boys served it faultlessly. His choir sang it beautifully. This was his first completed mission, but not his only one. Three others were being built. Many more had been planned up and down the Magdalena and the Altar Rivers. Father Kino allowed himself his moment of pride.

Outdoors, the women baked wheat bread and roasted great chunks of beef and pork and mutton. In the cookshade were stewed dried fruits from the mission orchards. The coffee was strong and sweet.

The Spanish sang the songs of Spain and danced the dances of Mexico. The Indians performed their age-old pagan ceremonies before the open door of the church to honor their Christian God. Later they feasted, sitting around the cookshade, helping themselves to meat and bread and salt.

In the church, before the statue of Francis Xavier, knelt Eusebio Francisco Kino, missionary Father to the Pima Nation. He knelt in a prayer of thanksgiving that God in His mercy had allowed him to carry the Faith to a foreign land.

The fiestas were a welcome time. They marked what had been accomplished and let the Indians of different tribes meet in peace and friendship. They gave overworked, lonely priests a chance to see others of their own race. They coaxed faraway reluctant tribes to come and see what had been done and perhaps to ask for a chance to do likewise.

But conversions, work, fiestas did not take up all the time. New trails had to be explored into an ever-widening land. By 1695 Father Kino had established a chain of new missions, in addition to San Ignacio, Imuris, Cocóspera and Remedios.

Establishing a mission meant days of riding in the saddle. From Dolores to the Gila country was a distance of probably two hundred miles. In 1697 the Padre made the round trip in thirty days, stopping at every village and rancheria to make friends with the Indians, instruct them, anoint them, and baptize the babies they offered for baptism. The next year he bettered this record, riding a thousand miles in twenty-six days. Year after year, for months at a time, he averaged more than thirty miles a day, often over new trails and always over dangerous ones. He rode with other Jesuit missionaries, with soldiers, with an Indian companion or two—but most of the time he rode alone.

He rode when the Indians were on the warpath, burning missions, martyring missionaries, killing soldiers—but he went safely along his chosen trails. He seldom approved of the manner in which the soldiers punished the Indians, and he was quick to express his disapproval. He loved his Indians as if they were his children, which in a way they were. He protected them whenever he could. Many times he rode at top speed all night to some place along the trail where, a runner had told him, an Indian was being harmed.

All the Indians of the Pimería Alta loved him for his gentle ways, and for his courage, and because he trusted them. In every way they could, they honored that trust. The very ones who had burned a Spanish village in anger drove a head of cattle a hundred miles, unsupervised, to a new mission because their Padre asked them to do so. But most of all the Indians loved Father Kino's sense of justice. If they were wronged, they knew that he would come to their rescue, if possible. If they wronged someone, they knew their Padre would expect them, if possible, to right the wrong or to make some reparation for it.

Because they loved him they obeyed him. If he was present when their anger flamed at some real or imagined injustice, he could calm them. If he told them to help the soldiers quell an enemy raid, they would do so willingly. The military depended on this and asked Father Kino to recruit for them when they needed Indian help. If he considered it a just cause, Father Kino obliged them.

So passed the years. A new century took its place in time. The year was 1700. How had the days and the months passed so quickly when there was so much left to be done? A new feeling of restlessness nagged him, pushed him. He must hurry, hurry. There was so much to do. Even before 1700 he had felt this compelling need to get things done.

On his last trip to the Gila he had been visited by a delegation of chiefs from the Yuman tribes along the Colorado River. They came to ask him to go and work in their territory. They brought him many gifts to show their affection and good will. Among them was a large blue shell.

Seeing the shell was a shock to Father Kino. Instantly he remembered the day he and Atondo had picked up such shells on the California coast of the Pacific. When was it? Fourteen years ago. He could not speak. Holding the shell in his hands, looking into its deep iridescent blue, he heard again the roar of the Pacific. Here in the desert, he smelled its salt. He felt again the joy of having reached the Pacific coast. But almost immediately this was followed by a feeling of grief. What had become of the California Indians? He had promised them he would return. Were they waiting for him?

Thoughtfully the priest turned the shell in his hand. Where had the Yuman chief found it? It must have come from the blue Pacific, and if it did there must be a land route to California. California then was not an island. He had never thought it was; a land route would prove his belief.

The fingers holding the shell tingled with excitement. Perhaps his California children would not be abandoned after all. Perhaps he could add them to his others in the Pimería Alta.

Father Kino questioned all the chiefs present about where such blue shells could be found, but the fact that the blackrobe was interested in the shell was more important to them than where it had been found. Each chief planned in his own mind how he would send his fastest runners for shells for the Padre. Their answers to Kino's questions were vague. They knew where to get them; they would get them for him. So the Indians planned how they would please their Padre by bringing him shells, and the Padre planned how, when he found out where the shells came from, he could use this knowledge.

His enthusiasm now was for finding a route to California by land. He added this to his other duties and dreams.

On Christmas Eve of the year 1699, Padre Eusebio had a visitor. Up the deep sand trail into Dolores rode the Jesuit Juan Maria de Salvatierra. Father Salvatierra had been missionary for ten years in a region to the south of the Pimería Alta. He had heard of Father Kino's miraculous success with the Pima Nation and had come to see for himself. Perhaps more than any other Jesuit of his time, Salvatierra was like Father Kino in his dedication and in his ways. The two priests became friends before the Christmas season was over.

First they visited some of the missions that had been established for some time: Remedios, Imuris, Magdalena, Tumacácori. Everywhere they stopped they were received with affection and pleasure. Arches covered with leaves were set up along their trails. The Indians came to meet them and take them to the church. Babies were given to them to baptize. The people waited eagerly for Mass and for the instruction that would take place afterward. Father Salvatierra saw everything and was impressed. He wanted to talk about the wonderful things that were happening at the missions, but Father Kino talked instead about the California Indians and about the blue shells and the possibility of a land route to California.

Everywhere they stopped, strange chiefs were waiting for them, asking them to come to their villages. At Tumacácori the head chief of the Sobaípuri settlement at Bac was waiting for them. Bac was a large and powerful settlement, and the chief had brought many of his people with him. It was a great occasion. They escorted the two priests to their village. Father Salvatierra wanted to stay, but his companion had to get back to Dolores. Before they left, however, he questioned the Indians about the blue shells. Their answers were vague. They, too, felt that where the blue shells came from was unimportant; what was important was to get shells for the Padre since he was so interested in them.

Later in the year Father Kino returned to

Bac, after having sent runners, as was customary, to announce his coming. He arrived at nightfall to be met by hundreds of Indians. Each one had brought him a blue shell as a gift. Some had come a great distance, from as far north as the Colorado River. Father Kino did not know what to do with the ton of shells that had been given him. If only he knew where they had been found! He looked at his shell pile ruefully, but, as was his way, he graciously thanked each Indian for his gift. They were delighted. Once again they had been able to give the Padre a gift from their hearts.

Father Kino continued to wonder and worry about a possible land route to California and to dream about what he could do if such a route existed. But while he wondered and dreamed he kept on with his building. In April of that year work was begun on the Church of San Xavier at Bac. Father Kino planned that it would be the largest and the most elaborate of his many mission churches. He himself dug its foundation.

When he was ready to go back to Dolores and his other missions, the chief at Bac gave the priest his own son. The boy—about twelve years old, his father said—was to go with Padre

Eusebio, to be his son and to learn from him all that he should know. This was the greatest gift the old chief could give his Padre—his son whom he loved, the pride and joy of his heart. Kino accepted the boy with deep humility, knowing the value of such a precious gift. And so the year continued, each day bringing to harvest that which had been planted, at the same time that fields were plowed and made ready for new planting.

It was in that year that the Padre reached the Yuma country for the first time. The Pima tribes had never been friendly with the Yuman. They did not speak the same language, nor did they look alike. The Yuman were taller, more powerfully built, and their skin was lighter. Their land was different and so were their ways. They distrusted one another because of all these differences.

Strange tales were told and rumors heard. Word reached Father Kino that some of the Yuman tribes killed and ate all strangers. He decided to go to see what the Yuman tribes were really like. He asked for Manje, a young military commander, with whom he had gone on California expeditions. They took eighty riding horses, ninety pack animals, eight packloads of provisions and many servants. They took along vestments and holy vessels for the celebration of Mass. A day's time before them, Papago cowboys drove about forty head of cattle. If the expedition was successful, a new mission would be established at Sonita.

When at last they reached the Yuma country they learned that the people were not cannibals, but friendly and eager to become Christians. Father Kino was not surprised; this was what he had expected. He established Sonita as his new mission base and planned the building of other missions at convenient distances from there. What did surprise him and fill him with joy was that on this trip he learned that he was above the head of the Gulf. California was joined to the mainland. It was not an island. Now he must find the overland route and build missions at convenient places along the way. This done, in time he would reach the California Indians.

In 1701 Tumacácori was completed, and the following year a mission was begun at Guévavi. Later that year Father Kino sent over seven hundred cattle across the Gulf to Loreto in California, where Father Salvatierra was now stationed. The herd that would be started would feed the Indians at the mission as well as furnish beef for the companies of soldiers that were constantly on the move quelling Indian uprisings and Apache raids. But Father Kino was never content to stop. Before one accomplishment was completed, a new one had begun. Before one dream was completely realized, a bigger dream was filling his heart and mind.

He had gone up and down, crossed and recrossed the vast Pimería Alta. In all he had made more than fifty journeys, each one from a hundred to a thousand miles in length. He had founded twenty-nine missions in the Pimería Alta and seventy-three *visitas*.

Chapter 11

FATHER KINO had explored the country, mapped it, helped make its history. He had been the first to record that history in his letters and diaries. Now, at the request of Father Gonzales, he began putting his diary in history form. Because he considered that everything he had been able to do was a favor of heaven, he called his record *Celestial Favors*. The manuscript was written in five parts at five different times in his life. He began it in 1699. He finished the fourth part in 1706. In 1710 he added a fifth part which was not a record of his work, but a plea to the King for more Jesuits to carry the Faith beyond the Pimería Alta.

As he wrote his *Celestial Favors*, Father Kino, for perhaps the first time in his life, treated himself to the luxury of looking into his memories. They were rich and many, small treasures bringing both laughter and tears as they flooded his heart. Today he let them come at will; tomorrow would be time enough to sort them into their proper places. For now, he would live them again, fingering each one lovingly, a bead in his rosary of time.

Not all of the memories were happy ones. Some were as sad, as bleak as a winter day when sand and sky and sea were wastes of hopeless gray. He thought of these times now, these cold times that chilled his heart with fingers of despair.

He still grieved over the needless death of young Father Saeta. He still missed him, though he had been martyred so many years

Priest to the Pimas

before. Father Francisco Xavier Saeta was from Sicily, the son of a family of noble blood. He had taken much of his training in Europe, but so eager had he been to begin missionary work among the Indians of North America that he had been allowed to come to Mexico to complete his training. After his ordination there had been many months of indecision before his assignment was made. He had so much to give and he was needed in so many places. At last he had been sent to work with Eusebio Kino in the Pimería Alta.

From their first meeting, Father Kino had felt close to the eager, young Jesuit. It was Kino who took him to Cabórica, which was to be his first mission. As usual, the Indians were overjoyed to see their Padre Eusebio, and when he told them that he had brought Father Saeta to stay with them, their joy knew no bounds. Looking forward to this day when they would have their own priest, the Indians had built a little house for their priest to live in. They showed this to him now, and Father Saeta was delighted.

The next day the young Jesuit began building his church. The Indians came to help him in such great numbers that he had to make hurried trips by horseback to all the near-by missions to beg for corn and wheat and beef to feed them.

Father Saeta had been a good beggar, as all Jesuits had to be, Father Kino thought as he turned the pages of his diary. Looking at the pages, he noted the long lists of his own gifts to the priest of Cabórica: a hundred head of cattle, a hundred sheep and goats as well as mares and their colts, packmules, pack saddles, wheat and corn, garden seeds, young trees for the new orchards. As he looked over the long list, he regretted that he had been able to give so little to the priest who had needed so many things in such a hurry. His time had been so short. He must have sensed it would be.

Father Saeta was so young, so enthusiastic, so dedicated. He loved his Faith and he loved his red children who received God's Word with such gentle hearts. "My children attend Mass every morning," he had written Father Kino and had gone on to tell of the work accomplished, the church completed, fields, gardens and orchards planted.

The young priest was working too hard, Father Kino had thought and had answered the letter with an invitation to visit Dolores at Eastertime. But Father Saeta had refused the invitation. He could not come. He could not leave his mission, his church or his children, even for a brief time.

Then trouble had started. It began at Tubutama, where an interpreter, an Indian from another tribe, had abused some Pimas who were working under his direction. The Pimas rebelled, and their rebellion spread like a grass fire across the sand wastes of the Pimería Alta. It spread from village to village. No white man nor the things he had brought with him were free from flaming anger of the Pimas on the warpath.

A runner brought Father Saeta word of the terrible things that were happening in neighboring settlements and missions. But Father Saeta was not afraid. Nothing would happen to his mission. His children loved him.

But it had happened. Father Kino, remembering what had happened, felt the salt of tears. He still grieved over the murder of the young missionary Father. Even now it was a knife in his heart when he thought of young Saeta receiving the arrows from the children he loved, clasping the crucifix to his heart and dying at their feet. After having killed the priest, the angered Indians had burned his house and his church. When the military had finally quieted them, soldiers went to Cabórica, where they found only the charred bones of the young nobleman from Sicily who had died as he had lived, adoring the God he served.

Father Kino remembered how he had ridden into the sand wastes to meet the soldiers who were bringing all that was left of Saeta to Dolores for burial. The old priest remembered. But now there was no anger in his heart—only grief, grief for the Indians who had killed their priest. After the savage fire of resentment had died in their hearts, they were again the gentle, childlike people Saeta had loved. A short time later Padre Eusebio had sent these same men, the ones who had shot the arrows into Father Saeta's heart, to drive a herd of cattle to a distant mission. They had willingly done so. They were glad to be of service and were grateful to be trusted again.

Remembering all these things, Father Kino shook his head. He must not dwell on bitter memories nor sad and evil days, although there had been many throughout the years. There had been better days and happier times, too. He must think of these times. Slowly the old priest turned the yellowed pages of his diary. Each page told a story, of tears, yes, but also of laughter. He smiled now, reading what he had written so many years before. It was an account of the time he had taken his little dog with him when he had visited some of his missions. Everything he did was always of interest to the tribes of the Pimería Alta. They would send runners from village to village telling the people that their Padre was coming, that he was alone or that others were with him, and that he would arrive in a certain number of days.

This time the runner must have told the children that their Padre Eusebio was bringing his dog with him. Ordinarily the Indian children were somewhat cruel to animals, but not to their Padre's dog. Anything that belonged to Padre Eusebio was special and to be treated with great respect.

Whenever Father Kino came to a mission, the trail was carpeted for many leagues with flowers and arches and marked crosses. All the Indians who lived near by came in great numbers to meet him, bringing gifts. This time, he remembered, something new had been added. The children came to greet and welcome his little dog. They brought it water and small baskets of pinole. They spoke gravely and politely to it, welcoming it to their village. Then they turned black, adoring eyes to their Padre Eusebio, asking him without words if what they had done had been pleasing to him.

Thinking back upon that day, Father Kino smiled gently. He loved all Indians because they were children of God, but especially he loved the little ones. He loved their ways. It made him very happy when they began to trust him and to follow him along the trail. Their ways pleased him. Where was it, he wondered now, what village was it where the little boys had been so delighted to learn that Padre Eusebio's horses ate grass instead of little boys?

Father Kino leafed the diary pages, reading a line here, a paragraph there. What a day that had been when the Indians had put him in a basket on a raft and had swam pushing the raft and its cargo, across the flooded Gila!

What a day it had been when he had first seen the great, imposing ruins of Casa Grande! There had been something about the empty, quiet, forsaken desert ruin that told more than any spoken word or written history about the grandeur of a people who had gone into eternity. Father Kino had said Mass in the great room where the massive clay walls had been polished by loving hands to marble smoothness. As he offered the Holy Sacrifice, the devotion of the kneeling Indians seemed to fill the desert air with reverence.

Father Kino closed his diary. Enough of remembering for this day. How good God had been to him, he thought, to have allowed him to bring the Faith to the New World desert, to bring the waters of Christianity to a parched land and to a thirsty people.

Padre Eusebio was now in his sixties. It had been a quarter of a century since he had ridden muleback from Vera Cruz to the City of Mexico. He was still as vigorous as ever. He rode as often and as long. He still fretted because time was passing. He was still restless, still in a hurry to make his dreams come true. There were so many. He dreamed of an overland route to California and the California missions opened and expanded. He dreamed of many Jesuit Fathers and many missions and many converts in the lands of the Yuman tribes. He dreamed of the conquest and conversion of the Apache and the extending of the Jesuit field in New Mexico, and he was still building missions throughout Pimería Alta, adding to the ones he already had built.

In March, 1711, he went to Magdalena to dedicate a new chapel at the mission there. The new chapel was to honor his patron, his beloved Saint Francis Xavier. There had never been a day of his life when he had not said a prayer to Xavier to ask him to obtain God's help for his servant, Eusebio Francisco Kino. There had never been an act in his life that he had not offered to God through the holy hands of Francis. So he rode to Magdalena this day in March. He blessed his people there and talked with them and listened to their troubles. He gave them faith and hope. Then, as he usually did, he spent the rest of the night in the church in prayer.

Morning dawned bright and gay. Nothing is so full of promise as March in Pimería Alta. The desert is abloom with desert flowers. The sun is mildly warm.

Magdalena was in a festive mood. The plaza before the church was dotted with arches. Needles from the pine trees of the mountains carpeted the ground in front of the church. Candles were lighted on the altar. Mass was begun. Padre Eusebio was getting old, but none of his flock noticed it. He was their Padre, giving them his time, his energy, his comfort, his love as he had always done.

Suddenly he became ill, terribly ill. The Indians helped him to the little room he always used when he came to see them. They laid him gently on his pallet with his saddle blanket for mattress, his saddle for pillow. A little after midnight God in his mercy called him to eternal rest.

He was rich in possessions: two coarse shirts, his rosary and his Breviary, and the love of thousands and thousands of his red-skinned children.

His life had been lived according to the prayer of Francis Xavier:

> ". . . to toil and not to seek for rest,
> to labor and not to seek reward,
> save that of knowing that I do
> Thy will, O God."

The day was March 15, 1711.

ST. AUGUSTINE ACADEMY PRESS

...because what children read really matters...

At St. Augustine Academy Press, we are dedicated to bringing you only solid Catholic literature from yesterday and today. To learn more, visit us online at

www.staapress.com

www.ingramcontent.com/pod-product-compliance
Lightning Source LLC
Chambersburg PA
CBHW031642040426
42453CB00006B/182